A SHORT HISTORY OF LAS VEGAS

A SHORT HISTORY OF

University of Nevada Press ▲▲ *Reno   Las Vegas*

VEGAS

Barbara Land and Myrick Land

FOREWORD BY GUY LOUIS ROCHA

The paper used in this book meets the requirements of American National Standard for Information Sciences— Permanence of Paper for Printed Library Materials, ANSI Z39.48-1984. Binding materials were selected for strength and durability.

University of Nevada Press, Reno, Nevada 89557 USA
Copyright © 1999 by University of Nevada Press
All rights reserved
Manufactured in the United States of America
Design by Erin Kirk New

Library of Congress Cataloging-in-Publication Data

Land, Barbara.
A short history of Las Vegas / Barbara Land and Myrick Land ;
foreword by Guy Louis Rocha.
p.   cm.
Includes bibliographical references and index.
ISBN 0-87417-326-4 (pbk. : alk. paper)
1. Las Vegas (Nev.)—History. I. Land, Myrick, 1922–1998.
II. Title.
F849.L35L35   1999
979.3′135—dc21   98-41746
CIP

08   07   06   05   04   03   02   5   4

Title page photo: Fremont and Main, viewed from the railroad depot, Las Vegas, circa 1931. Collection of Imre de Pozsgay, Reno Color Lab.

To the real Nevadans who introduced us to the real Las Vegas.

CONTENTS

ACKNOWLEDGMENTS

A complete list of individual names of people who provided lively stories for this book begins to look like a city telephone directory. They know who they are, and we thank them all. In museums and libraries, casinos and business offices, they cheerfully stopped what they were doing to help us find facts and pictures. For what we learned from their treasuries of information, we're especially grateful to:

Boulder City/Hoover Dam Museum; Clark County Heritage Museum; Colorado River Museum; Dickinson Library, University of Nevada, Las Vegas; Getchell Library, University of Nevada, Reno; Las Vegas Natural History Museum; Las Vegas News Bureau; Liberace Museum, Las Vegas; Lost City Museum, Overton; Nevada Commission on Economic Development; Nevada Historical Society, Reno; Nevada State Library and Archives, Carson City; Old Las Vegas Mormon Fort State Historic Park; Oral History Program, University of Nevada, Reno; Nevada State Museum and Historical Society, Las Vegas; Washoe County Libraries.

For personal reminiscences and clues to sources we'd never have found without their help, we thank Phyllis Barber, Bob Blesse, Myram Borders, Darrin Bush, Shayne Del Cohen, Caral Lee Conte, Ruthe Deskin, Mike Donahue, Phillip Earl, Ken Evans, Alan Feldman, Jake Highton, Robin Holabird, Christine Kelly, Jonnie Kennedy, Tom King, Don Laughlin, Joyce and Robert Laxalt, Janet and

Warren Lerude, Dennis McBride, Jennifer Michaels, David Millman, Peter Michel, Deborah Munch, Tommy Nelson, Irene Porter, Guy Louis Rocha, Rondi Roland, Karen Silveroli, Ron Stewart, Monique Laxalt Urza, Cathy War, and Valerie Wiener.

For their superb teamwork, endless patience, and encouragement when we needed it most, we thank the editors and staff of the University of Nevada Press.

Our thanks to Kirk Robertson for permission to quote from his poem "Driving to Vegas," published in *Just Past Labor Day: Selected and New Poems, 1969–1995* (Reno: University of Nevada Press, 1996). And to Writers Night Music (ASCAP) for the opening lines of "The Gambler," written by Don Schlitz, copyright 1977.

FOREWORD

This book is about my hometown. The town I grew up in, the town that grew up around me, the town that grew into a community that I barely recognize today; the town in Southern Nevada like every town and like no other town in the world: Las Vegas!

I was absolutely delighted when Barbara Land approached me about writing the foreword to *A Short History of Las Vegas*. While I had helped Barbara and "Mike" on this latest collaborative book project, directing them to resource material, reading chapters, and sharing the experience of being raised in the entertainment capital of the world, little did I know that my reward would be the chance to say something here about the city of my youth.

Maybe I first knew I came from someplace very different when I left Las Vegas for upstate New York and Syracuse University in 1969. Although I had visited Southern California as a child—I was born in Long Beach—it seemed to me then that there was something symbiotic between Las Vegas and Los Angeles–San Diego, and I certainly did not feel out of place there. In Syracuse, I encountered more humidity, snow, rain, and lush greenery than this denizen of the Mojave Desert had ever imagined. Much to my dismay, unlike my hometown, with its twenty-four-hour atmosphere, Syracuse—a city larger than Las Vegas at the time—virtually turned its lights off after midnight. I quickly found out what a novelty I was decked out in my white or green patent leather shoes, white belt, and warm-weather clothes. My fellow students from the northeast with their many accents (and I apparently without a dialect) did not know what to make of this street-wise kid from "Vegas."

"You live in Las Vegas? You're kidding. People don't live there. They go there. Where did you live? In a hotel?" I confronted questions practically every day that betrayed a perception of a city built on legalized vice and sin, absent families and children. The only image of my town was one long strip of casinos, hotels, and motels, and mobsters running amok.

"What did you learn in school?" (Like maybe kids growing up in Las Vegas trained to be bartenders, dealers, and prostitutes.) I told them there were PTAS, churches and synagogues, and service organizations. I explained that outside the hotel-casino complexes there were quiet neighborhoods with shopping centers, bowling alleys, parks, and playgrounds. They found what I had to say very hard to believe. How could a city like Las Vegas have anything in common with their hometowns? Even the more cosmopolitan students from New York City who appeared to grasp what I was telling them found it a stretch of the imagination. Remember, Atlantic City and other communities throughout the country had not yet legalized gambling. Nobody could grow up in Las Vegas and be "normal."

I thought I was reasonably normal. Yes, some of my classmates were the children of entertainers, Mob associates, and employees of Howard Hughes like Robert Maheu. Most of us did not have such credentials, however, and all of us were still "normal" kids who went to the movies, proms, sporting events, and cruised Main Street—in this case Fremont Street between the Union Pacific Railroad Depot and the Blue Onion Drive-In.

When I told my dormitory buddies that I had worked as a union busboy and dishwasher at the Nevada Club and the El Cortez Hotel, they were all suitably impressed and wanted to know if I gambled, drank, and went to the risqué lounge shows. I found it ironic that New York State's drinking age was eighteen at the time, and in Nevada we had to wait to twenty-one to legally consume alcohol.

Then there were all the questions about prostitution, especially the brothels. I did not understand the fascination with prostitution in Nevada. Even at my tender age I had heard of 42nd Street in New York City and Boston's "Combat Zone." Many Americans still view Las Vegas as aberrant. That perception has been tempered in recent years as millions visit the family-oriented theme park hotel-casinos, and as legalized gambling has spread throughout the nation. Yet when you read accounts of Las Vegas (Tom Wolfe, Hunter Thompson, Noël Coward, etc.), you realize that those on the outside do not experience what it is like to live on the inside. "Normal" people have been growing up and growing older in Las Vegas for generations, and Las Vegas has grown into one of the premier cities of the world.

In *A Short History of Las Vegas*, the Lands outline the Las Vegas story in its entirety, not just the glitz and glamour, the sensational and the sordid. This is a popular history that begins with the prehistoric era. We learn of the indigenous people before and after the coming of the European Americans. This lively and engaging work captures the trials and tribulations of a hardscrabble frontier inhabited by Mormons and other pioneers who many times clashed, sometimes cooperated with the native people (today members of the LDS Church and Native Americans are still very much a part of Las Vegas). The groundwork for the phenomenal transformation of southern Nevada in the twentieth century was laid with the completion of the last transcontinental railroad link in the nation and the founding of Las Vegas in 1905. However, some twenty-five years would pass before Americans recognized the difference between Las Vegas, New Mexico, and Las Vegas, Nevada.

Three events in 1931 forever changed the sleepy railroad town and Clark County seat of government: the construction of the massive Hoover (Boulder) Dam to tame the mighty Colorado River; the passage of a six-week divorce law; and the legalization of casino gambling. In a few short years Las Vegas had a fledgling resort industry, abundant electricity to power the growing town, and what seemed a limitless reservoir of water to quench the thirst of tourists and residents and transform the parched landscape into a neon oasis. The advent of the swamp cooler (I remember them well) and later refrigeration air conditioning revolutionized living in the desert. The Lands provide both colorful stories of a changing Las Vegas and an insight into what it took to build the infrastructure for a modern destination resort. Las Vegas, Nevada, was on the national map by the 1940s, and the Mob would help keep it there.

Some say mobster Benjamin "Bugsy" Siegel was the father of modern Las Vegas. The Mafia had infiltrated Las Vegas by the beginning of World War II, and Siegel's opening of the Flamingo Hotel on the embryonic "Strip" in December 1946 ushered in a new era of casino resort entertainment. Floor and lounge shows with famous Hollywood and vaudeville stars abounded. Topless revues, like *Minsky's Follies, Folies Bergere,* and the *Lido de Paris* became a mainstay at hotels beginning in the 1950s. Even Broadway productions graced the Strip showrooms (I remember seeing *Flower Drum Song* at the Thunderbird Hotel). Las Vegas soon went vertical, and new high-rise hotels gave the town an imposing skyline.

This era—so well portrayed by the Lands—beginning with Bugsy in the forties (who was gruesomely murdered in Los Angeles in 1947) and ending with Tony "the Ant" Spilotro in the eighties (Tony and his brother took "a dirt nap" in an Indiana cornfield outside Chicago in 1986) has shaped the public's image of Las Vegas. The distorted "Mob" image is what influenced the thinking of my fellow students at Syracuse University. Movies like the *Godfather* series, *Goodfellas,* and *Casino* have subsequently reinforced the negative stereotype of Las Vegas. The Mafia is no longer directly involved in running the casinos; corporate gaming has simply driven the Mob to the fringes of the gambling business.

Thanks to *A Short History of Las Vegas,* we know there is considerably more to the story. Like so many Nevadans of my generation, I was a product of the six-week divorce industry. My mother traveled to Las Vegas in 1955 with two toddlers in tow to untie the knot and stayed on. Those of us who were kids in the 1950s have fond memories of watching the atomic bomb explosions and the giant mushroom clouds rising into the desert sky. After the end of aboveground testing in the early sixties, we would suspend objects in our classrooms to see how far they would swing after a scheduled underground blast. And who could forget all the Las Vegas–Tonopah–Reno (LTR) buses loaded with thousands of workers every weekday snaking to and from the Mercury Test Site.

In the 1960s, Las Vegas and I both came of age. By the end of the decade, publicly traded gambling corporations had entered the scene. Howard Hughes and Kirk Kerkorian were the new gaming moguls shaping the face of the city. Las Vegas had eclipsed Reno as the nation's foremost casino, wedding, and divorce capital. Nevada Southern University, only fourteen years old, had been renamed University of Nevada, Las Vegas. And I had graduated from Clark High School, to return from Syracuse only for vacation breaks.

Las Vegas was my hometown, but it was no longer my home. While I was pursuing graduate studies in San Diego and Reno, Las Vegas was undergoing a tremendous metamorphosis. As late as the early 1980s it was still considered an adult playground, and Circus Circus, with all its carnival games and circus acts (which I enjoyed as a teenager), was an exception to the rule.

Today, thanks to Steve Wynn and others of the new breed of casino entrepreneur, the rule is colossal theme resorts loaded with family amusements. Where there was just one Strip on the old Los Angeles highway, now there is a Boulder Highway Strip and another emerging on the road to Tonopah. Downtown Las Vegas has been transformed into the canopy-covered, computerized light show called the Fremont Street Experience. Outlying Clark County areas like Mesquite, Laughlin, and State Line (now Primm) that were mere watering holes twenty-five years ago are megaresorts today.

Metro Las Vegas is big and getting bigger. At the current growth rate, two million people will inhabit the valley and environs early in the next century. Only the scarcity of water, and the expansion of other casino venues here and abroad, might slow this Juggernaut. I can never go home again, for, as Alan Richman says in "Lost Vegas" (*Gentleman's Quarterly,* November 1992), my hometown has changed like no other in the last twenty-five years.

The Las Vegas I knew lives only in my memory and in works such as *A Short History of Las Vegas.* Barbara and Mike Land, who collaborated in their writing for more than forty years, have produced a fitting tribute to my hometown. I pay tribute to the Lands, who have touched many lives, and now mine, during their distinguished careers as journalists and writers. Sadly, Mike died in 1998, and I witnessed the tremendous outpouring of love and heartfelt remembrance of this remarkable scholar and teacher at a ceremony held at the University of Nevada, Reno, Reynolds School of Journalism. I take great pride in having worked with Barbara and Mike on this handsome volume and excellent introduction to the "entertainment capital of the world." I only wish I had had a book like this to show my college classmates so many years ago.

Guy Louis Rocha, State Archivist
Nevada State Library and Archives

A SHORT HISTORY OF LAS VEGAS

New York–New York: Liberty lifts her torch beside a Coney Island rollercoaster against a towering Manhattan skyline—recreated on the Las Vegas Strip. (Las Vegas News/Bureau)

1

GREAT EXPECTATIONS

Driving down the Strip on a December afternoon in 1996, Las Vegan Muriel Stephens was showing her adopted hometown to a couple of visitors from back east. "Everything you see here," Stephens told her passengers, "was *not* here."

Remembering her own first impressions of Las Vegas, more than forty years earlier, Stephens pointed out some dramatic changes. "Where we are now," she explained, gesturing toward a row of glittering hotel-casinos, "there was nothing but dirt and desert."

"A pokey little poker town!" her guest remarked.

"Soon after we came here," Stephens confided, "my husband said, 'You know, when we get some money, we should buy a piece of property here.' And being an astute businesswoman, I said, 'Are you crazy? Who's going to want to live in the middle of this desert?'"

More than a million residents, most of them occupying quiet neighborhoods far from the Strip. And the more than thirty million visitors who come every year to sample the wonders of this unlikely spot in the Nevada desert.

Stephens's visitors were more than idle sightseers. Broadcaster Susan Stamberg and her assistant had come to Las Vegas to tape a segment for National Public Radio's *Weekend Edition*. They wanted to see it all, from the latest theme resorts to back streets and museums. If they had questions, their unofficial guide had answers. As a columnist for the *Las Vegas Sun*, Stephens had learned plenty of

"Probably no other metropolis in the world could boast of a resident populace who can remember when their town was founded."—Stanley W. Paher, *Las Vegas: As it began— As it grew*

inside stories. A resident since 1954, she had watched the city grow and change from a wild western outpost to a glittering fantasyland.

"There's the New York skyline!" Stamberg exclaimed as they approached the intersection of Tropicana Avenue and Las Vegas Boulevard. "Yes, there's the Chrysler Building . . . and the Brooklyn Bridge . . . and the Statue of Liberty . . . and Ellis Island. . . . All this way, and you end up in Manhattan!"

A few days later, in towns and cities across the United States, listeners to National Public Radio heard portions of Stamberg's taped interviews with Stephens and other Las Vegans, as well as her own ebullient comments.

"I'm waiting for Washington, D.C. [in Las Vegas]," Stamberg told the radio audience. "No White House yet, but there will be Paris, a new casino resort with an Eiffel Tower, going up on the legendary Las Vegas Strip to join New York–New York. . . . Across the street is the MGM Grand, a 5,000-room hotel designed like the Em-

City That Never Sleeps:
Flashing and shimmering, a constantly changing kaleidoscope of colored casino lights illuminates the Las Vegas nighttime sky. (Las Vegas News Bureau)

erald City. To get inside you formerly had to walk through a lion's mouth. Also on the Strip, a pyramid, a sphinx, some Camelot-ish castles that look more like the Kremlin, and a volcano that regularly erupts . . . big belches in the neon night."

Just a few blocks from this neon playground, as Stamberg was recording her comments, planeloads of visitors were arriving at McCarran International Airport. *More* visitors. Vacationers and gamblers, seekers of entertainment and seekers of luck, they keep on coming to explore the pleasure palaces.

Scattered among them are some who have come to stay. These are the new Las Vegans who will keep the city running and growing, not only for the millions of visitors but for their own families and descendants as well. Their taste for adventure has brought them here for reasons that separate them from the other risk-takers. They're here to build houses, open new businesses, treat hospital patients, teach school children, or work in the casinos.

They plan to become part of the city . . . maybe for a lifetime. Beyond the glitter of the casinos, these newcomers will discover a rich history that reaches back well beyond historic times. Perhaps they've inherited some of the frontier spirit of the early settlers in the Las Vegas Valley.

The Watering Place

Long before it was even a town—a railroad stop established in 1905—the place was called *Las Vegas*.

Spanish-speaking traders from New Mexico, on their way to California in 1829, strayed from the Old Spanish Trail blazed by Spanish missionaries in 1776. When they came upon springs of fresh water gushing out of the desert, they gave this unexpected oasis a Spanish name, *Las Vegas*, "the meadows," and added it to their

Las Vegas in the 1930s: "Relatively little emphasis is placed on the gambling clubs and divorce facilities—though they are attractions to many visitors—and much effort is being made to build up cultural attractions. No cheap and easily parodied slogans have been adopted to publicize the city, no attempt has been made to introduce pseudo-romantic architectural themes, or to give artificial glamor and gaiety. Las Vegas is itself—natural and therefore very appealing to people with a very wide variety of interests."—*The WPA Guide to 1930s Nevada*

"Arid Nevada is a phrase used only by those who do not know the state. . . . From the highest peaks to the lowest valleys, vegetation is abundant. It covers at least six life zones—the alpine, the sub-alpine, the yellow pine, the piñon juniper, the sagebrush, and in southern Nevada the creosote bush (Covillea). . . . So diversified is the State's topography that only a single hour of travel is needed from any of the larger towns to make the transition from the sagebrush to the creosote bush zones. . . . On Charleston Mountain, near Las Vegas, it takes less than an hour to pass from cactus and creosote bush to the alpine zone."—*The WPA Guide to 1930s Nevada*

x The big spring

The Big Spring: Fresh water gushing out of the desert was a welcome discovery for early travelers. Spanish traders called this unexpected oasis *Las Vegas,* meaning "the meadows." (Nevada Historical Society)

maps. Rafael Rivera, an adventurous young Mexican scout with Antonio Armijo's trading party, is named by most historians as the first European American to visit the Las Vegas oasis, but he and his companions were not the first people to drink from these springs.

Thousands of years before it had a Spanish name, the valley that became Las Vegas attracted thirsty travelers. As early as 11,000 years ago, some archaeologists believe, nomads camped at Tule Springs, just two miles west of modern Fremont Street. Crude stone tools and charred animal bones found in the area have been analyzed in twentieth-century laboratories to provide clues to the origins and survival methods of a forgotten people.

A vivid, imaginative portrait of these "first-comers" and their environment was written more than a half-century ago by archaeologist Mark R. Harrington, leader of several landmark Nevada excavations in the 1920s and 1930s. After he became curator of the Southwest Museum in Los Angeles, Harrington summarized the findings of twelve years of field work in a popular leaflet published jointly by his museum and Nevada's Clark County Historical Society.

"Ten or fifteen thousand years ago," he wrote, "at the close of the Pleistocene or Ice Age, the region we call southern Nevada, now so barren, was green and well-watered. Everlasting snow capped the higher mountains, from which flowed glaciers, living rivers of ice; blue lakes of fresh water dotted the lower valleys; streams were frequent where now only dry washes remain."

Harrington described a lush, wet landscape inhabited by huge animals, now extinct: mammoths, native horses and camels, giant buffalo, and "lumbering, stupid ground sloths, looking like imbecile, long-tailed bears." He imagined these vegetarian animals grazing along with elk, deer, mountain sheep, and antelope "not greatly different from those which still survive," threatened by meat-eating wolves, mountain lions, and saber-toothed tigers.

"Such was southern Nevada when man first set eyes upon it and found it good. Probably drifting in small bands from the north, where their forebears had crossed to Alaska from Siberia, these copper-hued, black haired discoverers of America hunted the grass-eaters and fought the flesh-eaters where never man had set foot before."

Like an archaeological jigsaw puzzle, built on scientific details mixed with speculation, Harrington's vision of the first Nevadans became more and more specific. He described their weapons and tools, supporting his reconstructed picture with evidence found buried in the desert.

"What these early people looked like we cannot say," he wrote, "for their bones have not yet been found; but we know they hunted the strange animals of the past and left the charred bones of elephants and camels slain for food in the ashes of their campfires; while in caves, their temporary stopping places, their weapons have been found buried with the remains of the ground-sloth. Traces of their camps, with heavily weathered implements of stone, may still

"The interpretation of ancient rock writings has intrigued many people; and there are wild speculations on the meaning of the symbols. Most of the interpretations, though, are mere romantic conjectures."
—Emory Strong, *Stone Age in the Great Basin*

In the Valley of Fire: "The rocks have been stacked, as though by a blackjack dealer, into huge sheets of carbonate rocks. This is the Overthrust Belt. The pressures from titanic forces have shoved rocks over rocks and stacked them into geologic puzzles."—Bill Fiero, *Geology of the Great Basin*

be seen on the former shorelines and headlands of streams and lakes long dry and forgotten, in districts where man cannot live today for lack of water."

When the water dried up, over a period of several thousand years, these nomads moved on, looking for food wherever they could find it. The archaeological trail becomes a little blurred between 9,000 and 4,000 years ago, but there's plenty of evidence of early human existence in the Las Vegas area. Archaeologists have named these prehistoric people for the places where their traces were first found: Tule Springs, Lake Mohave, Pinto Basin, Gypsum Cave.

Detectives of Time

Just fifteen miles east of Las Vegas, in the Frenchman Mountains, Gypsum Cave became the focus of worldwide scientific interest in the early 1930s when Mark Harrington and his associates announced their discovery of a skull unlike that of any known animal. A few years earlier, Harrington had visited the cave and noticed a deposit of strange animal dung. He knew it wasn't from a horse. Certainly not a modern horse. So what was it?

Suspecting, *hoping*, that he might have discovered traces of an extinct animal, Harrington organized an excavation party to begin work in January 1930. Soon after they started exploring, the expedition secretary, Bertha Pallan, found the odd skull in a crevice of the cave. When laboratory zoologists identified it as the skull of a long-extinct ground sloth, Harrington knew he was on the trail of an exciting find. Sloth bones and claws found in the cave confirmed the identification. If the researchers could find evidence of early *human* presence in the cave at the same time as that of the extinct sloth, they might be able to set an approximate date when these humans visited the cave.

Harrington's excitement over the sloth discovery soon attracted

Mark Harrington and his 1930 team of archaeologists found evidence of Ice Age humans living in Gypsum Cave, just fifteen miles east of Las Vegas. Six years earlier, Harrington had excavated an ancient "Lost City" he called Pueblo Grande de Nevada. (Nevada Historical Society)

financial and scientific support from the California Institute of Technology, the Carnegie Institution, and the Southwest Museum of Los Angeles. While these backers waited for detailed reports, the excavators began their meticulous digging, sifting, and recording. A few feet below the surface, they began to turn up traces of campfires, charred baskets, crystal ornaments, and fragments of tools used by early humans—maybe as far back as 1,000 B.C.—but not quite so early as the extinct sloth. The researchers kept on digging.

Finally, after excavating layers and layers of earth, sheep dung, and a rockfall three feet thick, hinting at a past earthquake, the archaeologists found what they were looking for. Eight feet below the original surface, buried underneath a solid layer of sloth dung, they came upon a fireplace and crude tools, convincing them that Ice Age humans had been in the cave about the same time as the extinct sloths. Cautiously, Harrington reported these discoveries as at least 7,500 to 9,500 years old. Years later, radiocarbon dating of Gypsum Cave samples found them much older, a treasury of archaeological evidence preserved in the cave for at least 10,000 years.

Some of the ancient artifacts uncovered by Harrington and his team are still displayed in the Southwest Museum in Los Angeles, along with the claws of the prehistoric sloth.

The Basketmakers

"Which would have been more startling to the Paiutes of two hundred years ago? Looking backward to the Pleistocene greenery and water—or forward to the bright lights and urban excesses of modern Las Vegas?"—Bill Fiero, *Geology of the Great Basin*

Look ahead a few thousand years to about 300 B.C. The climate has changed drastically. Lakes and rivers have dried up, the big animals have long since disappeared, and a hot, rocky desert surrounds the oasis that will become Las Vegas. Out in the desert, small groups of human hunter-foragers search for edible plants and small animals to feed their families. If they spot a bighorn sheep, they pick up their spears and pursue the animal with an efficient spear-throwing stick, now called an *atlatl*.

Sometimes a successful hunter stops to record his victory by drawing a picture of the sheep and his weapon, carving a design into the weathered surface of a desert sandstone cliff or canyon wall. Over the centuries, other hunters and travelers add their own artwork, to be found by European trailblazers in the eighteenth and nineteenth centuries and later to be interpreted variously by generations of archaeologists.

These ancient petroglyphs in the Nevada desert still puzzle scientists and historians. Some speculate that the drawings were more than casual graffiti—perhaps drawn by tribal shamans as ceremonial symbols. Others think they may be territorial markers or long-forgotten messages, weather reports, or public announcements. Experts disagree about the age of the drawings, but pictures of the atlatl could be very old indeed. Archaeologists have linked the

Ancient Graffiti? Or do these petroglyphs preserve vital messages scratched into rock surfaces by prehistoric artists? Archaeologists can only guess their meaning while studying them as important links to a past culture. (Special Collections, UNLV Library)

spear-thrower to the Basketmaker people, ancestors of the later Paiutes whose descendants still live and work in the Las Vegas Valley.

Basketmakers were named for the tightly woven baskets found in the remains of ancient fireplaces and pit-houses uncovered in Southern Nevada. Radiocarbon dating places the baskets at various times after 300 B.C., and researchers have reconstructed possible scenarios for the Basketmakers' lives:

Near one of the desert springs, a wandering band of hunters has set up a semipermanent camp. Each hunter has dug a shallow pit and has covered it with a roof of twigs and leaves supported by cut saplings. Women of the family sit outside these pit-houses, keeping an eye on the children while they weave baskets from grass and reeds. Some baskets are so tightly woven that they can be used to carry water from the spring. In a hollowed-out stone, a collection of seeds waits to be pounded into flour. Inside the shelter, in the middle of a bare earth floor, a fireplace is ready for cooking what-

"Petroglyphs are found on flat rock surfaces in many sections of the State; these designs were made by gouging the rock surface with tools fashioned out of harder materials such as quartz. The modern Indians can give no clue to the meaning of the symbols, and their interpretation has baffled all scientific investigators; they are not unlike the petroglyphs found in other parts of the world."—*The WPA Guide to 1930s Nevada*

ever the hunters may bring: a few rabbits, birds, or lizards. If they bring a bighorn sheep, the whole band will feast.

As long as they can find food, the band of Basketmakers keep their temporary pit-houses. In a lean year, they move on. When they discover better hunting grounds and another oasis, they may dig more pit-houses and stay a while. Archaeologists believe such shelters were common in the Valley of Fire, just fifty-five miles from the modern Las Vegas Strip, between 300 B.C. and A.D. 700.

Builders from the East

Toward the end of this period, the Basketmaker hunters had abandoned their atlatl spear-throwers in favor of a more sophisticated weapon. Bows and arrows were introduced by newcomers who had followed the rivers from an area now called Four Corners—where Arizona, New Mexico, Colorado, and Utah converge. When they came to a v-shaped valley where the Muddy River and Virgin River flowed together, these industrious people settled down, built strong adobe pueblos with many rooms, and planted crops.

Later called *Anasazi* (ancient ones), the pueblo dwellers brought with them the advanced skills of a highly developed culture still flourishing on the other side of the eastern mountains. They irrigated fields where they grew corn, squash, beans, and cotton. They made and decorated pottery, mined salt and turquoise, and traveled widely to trade with other tribes. For a time, they were permanent residents. Then suddenly, around A.D. 1150, the Anasazi abandoned their pueblos, leaving a mystery to puzzle archaeologists who would examine their traces centuries after the builders had gone.

Before Europeans came to this desert, pueblo dwellers and wandering basketmakers were not the only ancient people who shared the place. The Mohave people, and related tribes who migrated from Central America, settled in villages along the river banks where they built mud houses and simple brush shelters. They planted crops, caught fish, and often feuded with their neighbors, sometimes raiding rival villages and taking prisoners as slaves.

Indian slavery persisted, according to some historians, as late as 1860, especially among Ute tribes who sold Paiute women and children as domestic servants in New Mexico. In his pictorial history *Las Vegas: A Desert Paradise*, Nevada historian Ralph J. Roske wrote: "Spanish law forbade this slavery, but in the wilds of Utah and Nevada the law was flatly ignored. . . . After 1822, Mexican government officials proved to be as unable to stamp out the practice of Indian slavery as their Spanish predecessors had been. . . . Nor did the coming of the Americans to the area prevent slavery. . . . The settling of the Mormons in Utah did not fully discourage the Utes' practice of enslaving the Paiutes. Utah Territory passed a law in 1852 that banned slavery. This diminished the practice, but it continued. . . . Traces of the activity persisted at least until 1860."

First Visits to Mohave Country

A century earlier, Mohave villages south of Las Vegas were undisturbed by European outsiders until a Spanish missionary on his way to Los Angeles, Father Francisco Garces, paddled up the river in the 1770s. His encounter with the local people was peaceful.

So was the visit of Jedediah Smith, the first English-speaking explorer to record a meeting with Mohave Indians. In October 1826, about fifty years after Father Garces was received by Mohaves, Smith and his small party of mountain men traveled along the banks of the Virgin River to the Colorado. After four days of rough hiking through barren, rocky, mountainous country, Smith wrote, they found: "at this place a valley opens out about 5 to 15 miles in

"Perhaps the first written report of archaeological remains in Nevada came in 1827 in a letter from the fur trader and mountain man Jedediah Smith to William Clark, superintendent of Indian affairs. The letter simply informed Clark of Smith's discovery of a flint knife and a pipe in a salt cave in a mountain near the Virgin River."—Russell R. Elliott, *History of Nevada*

Jedediah Smith became the first American to enter what is now Nevada when he blazed a new trail along the Virgin River in late 1826, searching for beaver and a mythical river. (Nevada Historical Society)

width, which on the river bank is timbered and fertile. I here found a nation of Indians who call themselves Ammuchabas; they cultivate the soil, and raise corn, beans, pumpkins, watermelons and muskmelons in abundance, and also a little wheat and cotton."

Smith's report, addressed to General William Clark, Superintendent of Indian Affairs, was dated July 17, 1827. More than twenty years had passed since Meriwether Lewis and William Clark, commissioned by Thomas Jefferson, had completed their expedition across the continent to the mouth of the Columbia River. Their trail explored the northern wilderness, but the Southwest was still a mystery to Americans. Smith was eager to unveil that mystery.

"Sir," he wrote, "my situation in this country has enabled me to collect information respecting a section of the country which has hitherto been measurably veiled in obscurity to the citizens of the United States. I allude to the country S.W. of the Great Salt Lake west of the Rocky mountains."

Smith described the rugged terrain and his encounters with Indians. Buried in the report was a reference to salt caves along the Virgin River where he found stone tools, but this detail would wait nearly a hundred years before being "discovered" and the caves examined by archaeologists.

Three years after Smith's journey, Antonio Armijo and his Spanish-speaking traders followed a different route, some ninety miles to the north, and came upon gushing springs in the oasis they called *Las Vegas*. By 1844 Las Vegas appeared on many Spanish maps. The southwestern desert was still Mexican territory, but the U.S. Army Corps of Topographical Engineers was already at work on a systematic mapping program of its own.

An adventurous young officer, John C. Frémont, led a party of scientists, scouts, and observers into the Las Vegas valley on May 3, 1844. His journal entry for that day describes a camping ground called *las Vegas:* "a term which the Spaniards use to signify fertile or marshy plains, in contradistinction to *llanos,* which they apply to dry and sterile plains. Two narrow streams of clear water, four or five feet deep, gush suddenly with a quick current from two singularly large springs; these, and other waters of the basin, pass out in a gap to the eastward. The taste of the water is good, but rather too warm to be agreeable; the temperature being 71 in one, and 73 in the other. They, however, afforded a delightful bathing place."

When Frémont's report was published in 1845 ("printed by order of the Senate of the United States"), it carried a straightforward title: *Report of the Exploring Expedition to the Rocky Mountains in the Year 1842 and to Oregon and North California in the Years 1843–44* by Brevet Captain J. C. Frémont. His meticulous scientific observations, along with maps drawn by the German cartographer Charles Preuss, made the report a valuable reference—but the story of their adventures made it a bestseller in its time. Immediately, Frémont's work became a vital guide for explorers and pioneer settlers in the West.

Some of these pioneers followed Frémont's report and found the gushing springs in the oasis called Las Vegas. But Frémont's followers were unaware that ancient pioneers had settled not far away more than a thousand years earlier, centuries before any European had seen the American continent.

John C. Frémont described in meticulous detail "two singularly large springs" at a camping ground called Las Vegas, where his party of scouts and observers enjoyed a refreshing swim. (Nevada Historical Society)

The Lost City of the Anasazi

An article in the *New York Tribune* in 1867 reported the discovery of the "ruins of an ancient city" in Nevada. Investigators and writers began to call it "The Lost City." Surrounded by desert, the ruins were in a fertile valley where Mormon farmers from Utah were beginning to settle.

Archaeologists were interested, but science had to wait another fifty-seven years before anybody attempted a full-scale dig. Nevada Governor James Scrugham was interested, too. In 1924 he heard from John and Fay Perkins, two brothers from Overton, that they were living right next door to some ancient ruins. Scrugham seized the chance to organize a research team and called upon archaeologist Mark Harrington, the same scientist who would later discover remains of a prehistoric sloth in Gypsum Cave. With the support of the Smithsonian and Carnegie Institutions of Washington, D.C., they started digging.

Soon the scientists uncovered baskets, pottery, ancient weapons, animal bones, bits of blankets, all sorts of clues to the everyday lives of an ancient people. Most exciting of all were the buildings—pueblos—a complex of prehistoric "condominiums" that may have housed as many as twenty families. Harrington named the site

Ruins of an ancient pueblo, discovered long before scientific excavation began in 1924, were photographed by Mark Harrington at the Nevada site popularly called The Lost City. (Special Collections, UNLV Library)

Pueblo Grande de Nevada, but the press continued to call it The Lost City.

From their excavated clues, scientists began to reconstruct a detailed picture of the ancient civilization that once flourished in this valley. After ten years of careful, systematic excavation, the Harrington team felt they had just begun their research. Now their excavation site was about to be flooded, submerged under the waters of a new lake to be created by a huge dam on the Colorado River. The long-discussed Boulder Dam was already under construction, but the Franklin D. Roosevelt administration dispatched the Civilian Conservation Corps (CCC) to build a museum in Overton to house the precious collection of artifacts.

Harrington himself designed many of the exhibits and supervised CCC workers as they pitched in to help with the excavations as well. When it opened in 1935, the museum was operated by the National Park Service, but the Lost City Museum of Archeology was transferred to the State of Nevada in 1953. Today some 50,000 visitors a year find their way to the little museum on State Route 169, beyond the northern tip of Lake Mead, in the Muddy River valley near Overton. Inside and outside the building they discover the story of an ancient culture, vividly presented.

Museum staffers sometimes race with bulldozers in nearby Overton to rescue ancient artifacts before they are lost under new housing developments. Several universities, including the University of Nevada, Las Vegas, and the University of California, Riverside, have conducted archaeological field schools at the museum. They keep on learning more about the earliest settlers in what is now Clark County.

Modern visitors are fascinated by the reconstructed portrait of this early civilization, but nineteenth-century settlers considered themselves the first to tame an ancient wilderness. They followed more contemporary trails or blazed their own.

Q: What Nevada county was once part of Arizona?

A: Clark County in southern Nevada was part of the Arizona Territory until 1867.

—Richard Moreno, *The Nevada Trivia Book*

The Old Mormon Fort, built of sun-baked adobe bricks in 1855, is believed to be the oldest non-Indian structure in Southern Nevada. This 1930s photograph shows the only surviving part of the original fort, later protected by the Nevada Division of Parks. An ambitious rebuilding of the whole fort was begun in 1998. (Nevada Historical Society)

2

THE SETTLERS

Traveling from Salt Lake City to the California coast in 1852, Mormon missionary Hosea Stout and his companions stopped for water at the Las Vegas Spring. They had followed the old familiar Spanish Trail, except for a few shortcuts and diversions described by John Charles Frémont and other recent travelers. Now, just eight years after Frémont's first visit to the spring, the Mormons were using his detailed maps of a route that had become especially useful to California-bound wagon trains. Las Vegas was not yet a settlement, but the oasis was a welcome rest stop along the way.

Stout recorded his brief visit in his diary on November 19, 1852: "We . . . encamped at the head of Los Vagus which is formed of a boiling Spring of pure water about blood heat. This Spring is some 20 feet in diamiter, of a circular form, the water about 2 feet deep, the bottom quick sand, boiling and heaving up like thick boiling soup, as the water forces its way through it."

A meticulous diarist, Stout entered his notes every day, no matter where he was, even in the middle of a desert. Like Samuel Pepys in seventeenth-century London, Stout wrote about small details that might have seemed boring or trivial to his contemporaries. He also recorded his observations of important happenings in the Mormon organization. Later scholars, attempting to reconstruct and interpret Mormon history, have found Stout's everyday reporting as valuable as his descriptions of momentous events.

As early as December of 1847, Porter Rockwell led a party of fifteen men to California to buy provisions and livestock for the Mormon settlement at Salt Lake. They made the trip along the Old Spanish Trail and returned to recommend the route. As others followed the trail, stopping by the Las Vegas spring, they brought back detailed descriptions.

When he first saw Las Vegas, Stout was on his way to China to spread the word of a controversial new religion. The Church of Jesus Christ of Latter-day Saints had been founded just twenty-two years earlier, based on revelations reported by the prophet Joseph Smith and recorded in The Book of Mormon, published in 1830. Since then, Smith and his followers—the growing company of Saints—had moved around from New York to Ohio, Missouri, and Illinois, often pursued by state militia and angry mobs who objected to the Mormon recruitment of converts and, later, to their polygamous lifestyle.

By 1844, Smith felt confident enough to declare himself a candidate for the presidency of the United States. A month later, he was jailed in Illinois and shot by militiamen. After his death, the Saints found a new leader, Brigham Young, who would lead them west to the Promised Land.

Hosea Stout was an early convert, one of the Saints. At various times he had been an officer in the Mormon militia and the law enforcement chief who kept order among any unruly Saints as they struggled toward the City of Zion. When the Mormon pioneer company reached the Salt Lake Valley in July of 1847, they had left the United States for a region still held by Mexico. The two countries were at war, but Brigham Young and his Saints were convinced that they had found their Promised Land.

A few months later, the war with Mexico ended and the United States Senate accepted the Treaty of Guadalupe Hidalgo on February 2, 1848, ceding all Mexican territory north of the Gila River to the United States. This included all the land that later became Utah and Nevada.

Brigham Young had ambitious plans for a huge new Mormon State of Deseret in the same area. Hosea Stout would be its attorney

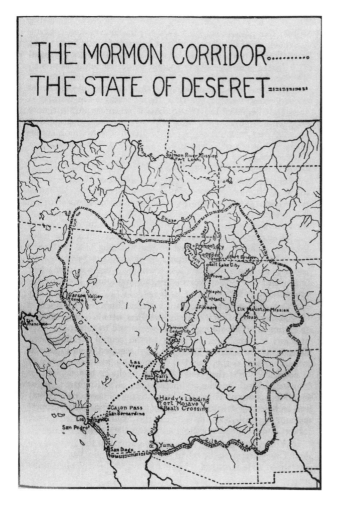

THE MORMON CORRIDOR⋯⋯⋯⋯○
THE STATE OF DESERET▪▪▪▪▪▪▪▪

Brigham Young had a dream of Deseret, a new nation to be created in the western wilderness with his band of Mormon Saints. Instead, he became governor of the United States Territory of Utah. (Special Collections, UNLV Library)

Scattered settlements planned by the Mormon Church in the 1850s expanded Mormon influence beyond Utah into New Mexico, Nevada, Arizona, and California. (Special Collections, UNLV Library)

By 1849, wagonloads of California-bound emigrants were passing through Salt Lake City, stopping to check their maps and stock up on food for the long journey across the desert. If they needed a guide, Jefferson Hunt was ready to help. As a leader of the Mormon Battalion and an experienced trail guide, he promised to show them a much safer route than the Death Valley crossing many had planned. That year, Hunt led a train of 107 wagons through Las Vegas to California, charging each wagon ten dollars for his services. A year later, the Mormon Trail had become a busy highway for wagon trains, and the Las Vegas spring was a popular rest stop.

"The valley is extensive and . . . by the aid of irrigation [could] be highly productive. There is water enough in this rapid little stream to propel a grist mill . . . and oh such water! It comes just at the termination of a 50 mile stretch without a drop of water or a spear of grass. Pah Eutahs here in great numbers, but they run from us like wild deer."
—Addison Pratt in his diary, 1848

general. By the time Stout visited Las Vegas on his way to China, Deseret had been absorbed into the new United States Territory of Utah, and Brigham Young was the Utah governor. Las Vegas, in what is now Southern Nevada, was part of the Territory of New Mexico. As a trusted apostle of Governor Young, Hosea Stout kept his eyes open for opportunities to expand Mormon influence into New Mexico and California.

By this time, the Mormon Church was planning a string of settlements between Salt Lake City and the Pacific Coast. The new village of San Bernardino, founded in 1851, already had become a regular stop for travelers to Los Angeles. Stout may have seen similar possibilities for Las Vegas when he described it in his diary: "This is the first stream, since we left the basin, which I have seen that could be used for irrigation, or where the Soil would produce any thing for the use of civilized man. . . . Here we found the wild cabbage, evidently the original of the tame; also grape vines in abundance presenting the appearance of an old dilapidated vinyard. The grape vines, the luxuriant soil in the extensive valley, all conspire to make this a most desirable spot for man to be."

The grapevines could have been cultivated by Indian residents in earlier times, but Stout didn't speculate about that. In his journal he preserved his feeling about this "desirable spot": "Like the oasis of Arabia, the weary traveller can here set down a calm repose & rest himself, after passing the parched desert."

Less than a month after Stout wrote those words, Las Vegas became a regular stop on the winter mail route between Salt Lake City and California. In the spring of 1854, the U.S. Congress established a regular monthly mail service along that route and appropriated twenty-five thousand dollars to build a military road. For Brigham Young in Salt Lake City, the time seemed exactly right for building a Mormon settlement at Las Vegas—roughly halfway between the Utah capital and Los Angeles.

On April 6, 1855, Young called thirty men to go to Las Vegas, with William Bringhurst as their leader. Their assignment was to "build a fort there to protect immigrants and the United States mail from the Indians, and to teach the latter how to raise corn, wheat, potatoes, squash and melons."

The Paiutes had been planting and growing crops in the area for centuries, but many of European descent still considered them savages, in need of instruction and conversion. The Indians had plenty of reasons to be suspicious of white men, after unfriendly encounters with earlier travelers, but Bringhurst and his Mormon missionaries were ready to treat them fairly.

Accompanied by his thirty men, forty ox-drawn wagons, fifteen cows, and several horses, Bringhurst completed the trip from Salt Lake City in thirty-five days. As soon as they reached the Las Vegas Valley, June 14, 1855, the leaders explored several sites before selecting a hilltop about four miles east of the Springs.

By the end of the summer they had cut away acres of mesquite, planted crops, and started building a fort with sun-baked adobe bricks they had made on the spot. They cleared a wagon road to the nearby mountains, where they cut down trees for logs to build cabins near the fort. Everybody worked diligently while Bringhurst supervised the jobs to be done, led sermons and prayers, and kept in touch with Mormon headquarters in Salt Lake City.

Letters from Las Vegas

For almost two years, Bringhurst sent regular reports from the fort. Less than a month after the party arrived at Las Vegas, he ac-

In the summer of 1850, an advertisement in the *Deseret News* informed travelers that Elijah Ward of Salt Lake City would escort wagons to California settlements for the standard ten-dollar fee. For the same price he would guide a company of five footpackers or anyone with pack animals.

knowledged the help of his Paiute neighbors in a letter dated July 10, 1855:

Shortly after we arrived here, we assembled all the chiefs and made an agreement treaty with them for permission to make a settlement on their lands. We agreed to treat them well, and they were to observe the same conduct towards us, and with all white men. Peace was to be preserved with all emigrants traveling through this country, as well as with the settlers. If travelers through this country will use the Indians well, there will be no trouble with them, but if they are mistreated, they are ready and able to take revenge on the first opportunity. They recount many instances of unprovoked murder committed by white men who have traveled this road, but are now willing to bury all animosities and to once more try the conduct of white men.

For the most part, Mormons and Indians worked together harmoniously during the building of the fort. Sometimes there were misunderstandings about property ownership—who owned certain tools or food—since the Indians were accustomed to sharing, but disputes were often settled with the help of the mission's clerk and interpreter, George W. Bean. The twenty-four-year-old Bean considered himself a friend of Indians in Utah. When he had lost an arm in a cannon explosion, sympathetic Indians had visited him, taught him some of their language and learned English from him. Now, at the Las Vegas mission, Bean was Bringhurst's trusted deputy, responsible for corresponding with President Young and keeping records of travels and daily activities.

Decades later, Bean's diaries and letters were given by his daughter, the late Flora Bean Horne, to the Daughters of Utah Pioneers.

In 1994 the Clark County branch of DUP published a little booklet, *The Las Vegas Fort*, containing biographical notes about the original settlers and excerpts from some of their letters and diaries. Bean's detailed account of life at the fort reflects a superior attitude toward the Paiutes, but at least he gives them credit for the work they did: "The Indians were soon partially converted to habits of industry, and helped us to grub the land, make adobes, attend the mason and especially to herd the stock. They were fairly honest and soon joined the Church. During the summer most of the adults were baptized and in many ways showed improvement. They herded the Emigrants' teams as they stopped on their way to California. They irrigated our land and assisted in . . . construction of a fourteen foot wall around a space of one hundred and fifty feet square, which constituted our mission fort."

During the first winter, when some of the settlers returned to Salt Lake City, Bean was among the small group who stayed at the fort. "We who remained were seventeen in number and probably one thousand Indians within sixty miles, but we had made considerable progress in civilizing those near us and we trusted in the Lord."

Bean received instructions to take a census of "all Natives within the boundaries of our Mission field," giving him a chance to explore, observe, and learn more from the Indians. Before long he was reporting valuable discoveries: tall ledges of crystal salt near the Virgin River, good timber in the mountains, and what appeared to be extensive lead deposits less than twenty miles west of the fort.

When Bean reported the lead discovery to Brigham Young, the Mormon president sent Nathaniel V. Jones to look at the mine and to organize the Las Vegas settlers and missionaries to get the ore out and ship it to Salt Lake City. Bean's later account said Young hoped the lead "would be useful for tools and bullets, as pioneers had a few molds."

Trouble at the Mine

Within a year the lead mine was producing ore, but Jones reported it was "very hard to smelt." When workers tried to pour the stuff into bullet molds, the results were uneven, and the bullets easily cracked. The amateur miners didn't realize that they weren't working with pure lead at all. What they had found was galena ore carrying silver. Without recognizing this treasure, they kept on shipping "lead" until Young told them to abandon the mine, leaving the unsuspected silver for later geologists to find.

Even before the disappointment of the bullets, the missionary miners faced other problems. According to Bean, "some discontent soon sprang up between the strict rule of President Bringhurst and the liberal ideas of some of the newcomers who were supported by N. V. Jones and his lead workers." Bean and three other missionaries were called to Salt Lake City in September of 1856 to report the situation to Young. Each man was accompanied by a ton of lead ore hauled by four mule teams. They made their report and Young gave his decision: "After many questions asked by President Young, he realized the spirit of the Mission was broken and he thought best to abandon it, but to get all the lead possible before this Mission went out. Then suggested that the families could return to the settlements, and the boys with teams haul as fast as possible, until the lead was worked out. This was late in 1856."

By the end of January 1857, the mine was abandoned. A month later, a letter from Young gave the Mormon brethren permission to leave the fort, officially closing the Las Vegas Mission. Back in Utah, facing trouble with the federal government, Young was calling faithful Mormons to rally at the Great Salt Lake. A few settlers stayed at Las Vegas for a few more months to harvest the crops.

What happened next seems to indicate that this skeleton crew ignored or forgot Bringhurst's advice about respecting the Indians.

When harvest time came, their Paiute neighbors—disillusioned by the treatment they were receiving—swept in and carried away the whole crop. This was the last straw for the remaining settlers. It was time to pack up and go home.

"Dear Companion"

Among the documents preserved by the Daughters of Utah Pioneers are some domestic messages, less literate than those written by Mormon leaders, that provide vivid insights into the lives of lonely men who missed their families. During the earliest days of the Mission, Aroet Lucius Hale scrawled a hurried letter to his wife, Olive. Under the dateline, "Los Vegus New Mexico, July the 10, 55," he wrote without punctuation, spelling words as he heard them: "Dear Companion it is with gratest pleasuer that I agin Wright to you I am well & hope that these few lines will finde you & the Chrildren injoying the Same Blessing this is the 5 Litter that i have Sent to you and have recived non but expect to this Male. I want to here from you very mutch & how you & the Chrildren are gitten a Long."

After a few words about his health and the work being done by the mission, Hale asks Olive to send him a picture of herself and the children: "You Wanted me to take your Derguerritype Likeness with me but I refused to do So I tell you what I Wood like now if you are properd and the way Should be opened for you & you Could do it and not distress you Selves that is your Likeness and the Chrildrens in one Groop these I would except Without much ergin."

Hale observes that other men at the mission have pictures of their wives and children and he doesn't want to be left out. After all, "I have you as good Looking a Woman as eny of them." He reminds

"Nevada has long been a means to an end. Part of its destiny is to be a thorofare for Americans eager to get across. The faster the better. . . . Nevada history has been made, to an extraordinary extent, by groups of temporary residents eager to depart."
—Richard G. Lillard, *Desert Challenge: An Interpretation of Nevada*

Olive to put on her "Fineups" for the photograph and to borrow some jewelry. After a few more lines of advice and family business, Hale makes one more request. As a faithful Mormon, he is entitled to more than one wife, and he has a new bride in mind. He asks Olive to help him woo her: "If Azro don't take Mary this time I want you to Spark her for me if you Cant get her I want you to try and git Some other good one Git a holesolm mormon for I will not have nother One. I am bound to have one as Soon as my Misheon is ended."

Reminding Olive to relay his greetings to friends and neighbors, Hale ends his letter: "I must Close my Letter by Saying may the Lord prosper you & open the way for you that you may be Blest With helth & the Comforts of life is the Prair of your Companion Aroet L. Hale."

Cabins and stockades built by the Mormons and their Indian workers remained at the deserted fort, welcome shelter for carriers of the Overland Mail and other travelers to and from California. During the Civil War, several California newspapers reported that the old Mormon fort was to be renamed Fort Baker, a new military post for four companies of Union soldiers. As it turned out, the story had been deliberately and falsely planted by Colonel James H. Carlson, Commander of the First California Volunteers, to deceive Confederate spies. Still, some later writers picked up the news stories and preserved the false history of "Fort Baker."

A detailed account of Carlson's strategy is given by Stanley W. Paher in *Las Vegas: As it began—As it grew.* Paher concludes that "Fort Baker fulfilled a mission for Carlson by diverting attention from his march through southern Arizona during a critical time in the Civil War. The abandoned Mormon fort buildings garrisoned no troops; there were no bugle calls, no fighting, no improvements made."

The Old Las Vegas Mormon Fort became a State Historic Park in 1992, and archaeologists began digging around the foundations. Two years later, the Archaeo Nevada Society joined Louis Berger and Associates in a field school to teach interested amateurs the basics of archaeology, including excavation techniques and laboratory processes. A park brochure traces the fort's history from 1855 to the present.

The Paher book is a treasury of old photographs, sketches, and maps accompanying a text based on tireless research in libraries and newspaper files. Paher also tracked down early Las Vegans whose parents were in the valley as early as 1880. Two of these, Fenton M. Gass and his sister Lelah Vegas Gass Slaughter, were in their nineties when Paher interviewed them. Both recalled a childhood on the Las Vegas ranch owned by their father, Octavius Decatur Gass, an educated Ohio native who moved into the abandoned Mormon mission and turned it into the first lasting settlement in the valley.

Vegetables and Vineyards

During the California Gold Rush, Gass had traveled to San Francisco and later to Los Angeles, where he became an irrigation inspector. In the 1860s he filed a few mining claims in Eldorado Canyon, but never struck a bonanza. By 1865 Gass was ready to try his luck as a rancher. His friend William Knapp owned a little property near the old Las Vegas fort where he planned to run a store for travelers on the Mormon Trail. Gass looked at the area and found it promising; then he invited two fellow prospectors to join him as partners in a ranching venture.

The men took over the deserted Mormon fort, rebuilt it, and cultivated the weed-infested fields. They restored the adobe brick buildings and made them the nucleus for their "Los Vegas Rancho," spelled with an "o." Making use of his experience in Los Angeles, Gass constructed irrigation works on the ranch. Before long the partners were irrigating four hundred acres of land.

They grew wheat, oats, and barley, hiring Paiute workers to harvest the grain. After the first harvest, they planted cabbages, onions, potatoes, beets, and melons. Over the years their fruit trees blossomed and produced figs, apricots, apples, and peaches to be sold to travelers. Wagon trains rolled up to the gates, sometimes staying as long as a week to rest and buy supplies. When visitors tasted the wine Gass produced from his own vineyards, they spread the word that Las Vegas was the best rest stop on the trail.

Eventually, Gass bought out his partners and expanded his ranch to 640 acres. After his 1872 marriage to Mary Virginia Simpson, daughter of a wealthy Missouri farmer, Gass added new buildings, including a spacious ranch house for his bride. She ran the house on a grand scale, by desert standards, with Chinese and Bavarian cooks in the kitchen. Paiute house servants did the cleaning and laundry. Mrs. Gass loved to sew, and she taught some of her employees to make their own clothes. Some visitors thought her a bit eccentric when they saw her pick up a shotgun to drive hawks away from her chickens, but they marveled at her steady aim. The Indian servants nicknamed her "sharp eye."

Even before his marriage, O. D. Gass had become a political figure in the new Arizona Territory, where he served four consecutive terms as a legislator. Since he spoke Spanish and several Paiute dialects, Gass was especially adept at communicating with Indian and Mexican leaders.

Las Vegas had been part of territorial New Mexico when the Mormons built their fort in 1855, but the western segment of the territory became Arizona in 1863, when the new state of Nevada was created. Las Vegas was part of Mohave County, Arizona, when Gass acquired the land. As a legislator, he backed a bill to slice off a piece of Mohave to create Pah-Ute County, bordering on the new state of Nevada. When federal mapmakers gave Nevada a triangular portion of Arizona west of the Colorado River, the Las Vegas ranch was in disputed territory and Gass was still an Arizona

Old stage house Arrowhead Trail, Las Vegas Nevada.

Las Vegas Creek flowed through a shady oasis on the old stagecoach route from California in the early days when Las Vegas was still a dusty town on a railroad track. (Special Collections, UNLV Library)

First Rancher: Ohio-born Octavius Decatur Gass failed to find a fortune in the gold mines of California, but his vision of agricultural riches paid off when he moved into the abandoned Mormon Fort and created his first successful ranch in the Las Vegas Valley. (Nevada Historical Society)

leader. By the time he and Mary Virginia were married in Pioche on February 24, 1872, the dispute had been settled and they were citizens of Lincoln County, Nevada.

Unfortunately for Gass, the state of Nevada intended to collect back taxes from former Arizonans in that part of the state. Paher's Las Vegas history chronicles in detail the ups and downs of the Gass family and their ranch. Everyday happenings, recalled decades later by the surviving children, provide a picture of a cheerful, busy household where visitors were always welcome. One of Paher's many rare illustrations is a photocopy of three pages from the ranch-owner's day book. Among other specifics, he recorded notes about the weather, his children, the cost of food and tobacco, and a tax bill for 1877.

Maybe extravagance was to blame, or poor management, or maybe it was just hard luck, but by this time Gass was in debt, looking for a way to save the ranch or sell it. He took a chance in August 1879 and borrowed five thousand dollars in gold from Archibald Stewart, a prosperous rancher and businessman who lived in Pioche. A year later, when the note came due with interest, Gass couldn't pay. A nine-month extension didn't help, so Stewart acquired unencumbered title to the ranch on May 2, 1881.

The Las Vegas ranch prospered under its new management. At first, Archibald Stewart intended to operate the property at a distance, with the help of two partners. Stewart and his pretty wife Helen were comfortably settled with their three children in Pioche, and their business was thriving. But the partners disagreed and split up the business in the spring of 1882. Stewart moved his family to the Las Vegas ranch, planning to make it their temporary home while he managed the ranch and reorganized his other enterprises. As it turned out, they never moved back to Pioche. A

little more than two years after the Stewart family arrived at the ranch, Archibald Stewart was dead.

The Stewart Ranch, after the death of Archibald Stewart, was run by his widow, Helen, with the help of Paiute and Hispanic workers. (Special Collections, UNLV Library)

Who Killed Archibald Stewart?

On a hot July afternoon in 1884, Helen Stewart was at home with her four children, trying to keep them cool. She was pregnant again and avoided doing anything strenuous, but when she saw a man on horseback approaching the house she went out on the porch to greet him. The rider had brought a note from Conrad Kyle, a neighbor who owned a ranch two miles from the Stewart property. The message was brief and blunt: "Your husband is here dead. Come take him away."

At first, Helen couldn't believe the note, but she immediately saddled her horse and rode to the Kyle ranch, where she found Archibald's body outside the house, covered with a blanket. Her farm hands put the body in a wagon and carried it home. Devas-

First Lady of Las Vegas:
The honorary title came after her death, but Helen J. Stewart earned the respect of her neighbors, employees, and casual visitors. As a widow with five children she operated a 2,000-acre cattle ranch and farm, becoming the largest landowner in Lincoln County. A close friend described her as "a tiny Dresden China piece of femininity." (Nevada Historical Society)

tated, she watched them bury her husband as she read aloud the burial service from the Book of Common Prayer.

While she waited for the law to arrive from Pioche, Helen Stewart grew more and more skeptical about the story she had been told of Archibald's death. Conrad Kyle said he had been away at the time of the shooting. Schuyler Henry, a ranch hand once employed by Stewart, said that he had killed his former boss after Stewart had fired at him first. It was a matter of self-defense, Henry claimed. Helen didn't believe him. She was convinced that more than one man was responsible for her husband's death.

Thirteen days later, when the sheriff came to investigate, Helen said she suspected Conrad Kyle (whose name was also spelled Keil or Kiel) of concocting a plot to kill her husband with the help of Schuyler Henry and Hank Parrish, a notorious gunfighter. Parrish had been on the Kyle ranch when Stewart's body was found but had left by the time the sheriff arrived. Eventually, August 11, 1884, a grand jury in Pioche heard testimony from Kyle, Henry, and Helen Stewart. Parrish couldn't be found. (Six years later, he was found guilty of another murder.) The jury accepted Henry's self-defense claim and voted sixteen to one to dismiss charges against Kyle and Henry.

What really happened? Over the years, the story has been told and retold with many speculations and variations in detail. One plausible scenario is offered by Stanley Paher in his history of Las Vegas. According to Paher, Archibald Stewart and Schuyler Henry had been quarreling for some time before the ranch hand finally walked off the job and went to work for Conrad Kyle. Stewart, who was away from the ranch when Henry left, was furious when he returned and found out what had happened. Stewart grabbed a rifle and headed for the Kyle ranch, telling Helen he intended to shoot a steer.

Edwin and William Kyle, quarrelsome sons of pioneer rancher Conrad Kyle, were found dead of gunshot wounds on October 11, 1900. A coroner's jury called it murder-suicide. When their bodies were exhumed more than seventy years later, UNLV scientists declared it a double murder. (Special Collections, UNLV Library)

Vacation Destination:
Travelers found hospitality at
Helen Stewart's ranch-resort
before she sold it in 1902.
Could they imagine the neon
glitter of a future Las Vegas?
(Nevada Historical Society)

"I remember Helen J. Stewart
very well. She was a charming
little old lady. She had quite a
lot of education for her day
and she was very hospitable.
Of course, she welcomed travelers. She said that . . . when
they were coming from the
north she could see them
coming across the desert and
would hurry and put coffee on
and a pan of biscuits in the
oven. . . . People would come
and camp for two or three
days, and the longer they
stayed the better she liked
it."—Florence Boyer, Oral
History

Drawing from several earlier accounts of the killing, Paher describes Stewart's furtive approach to the house where Henry was
sitting near an open window. When Henry spotted the man with a
gun aimed in his direction, he hopped to his feet, picked up a rifle,
and the two men shot it out. Paher adds, "Everyone in the area believed that Henry killed in self-defense. Not much sympathy was
expressed for Stewart, and many believed that he was an overbear-
ing man who had met his just deserts."

More than a century after the killing, the jury's verdict still
stands. A later account of the case appeared in Ralph J. Roske's *Las
Vegas: A Desert Paradise*, a 1986 pictorial history of the city. Roske,
a professor of history at the University of Nevada, Las Vegas, discovered that Archibald Stewart's body had been exhumed in the
1970s "for another reason" and examined by two UNLV anthropol-
ogists, Richard Brooks and Sheilagh Brooks.

"They hoped to find a clue as to how Stewart died and who
killed him," Roske reported. "All that could be determined on
the site, without more time and a laboratory examination, was that
Archibald Stewart was killed by a bullet to his right cheek which
went through his skull and exited from the back of his head."

Roske concluded, "the mystery remains unsolved—and perhaps unsolvable."

Helen Stewart was never satisfied with the jury's verdict, but she carried on the business of the Las Vegas ranch for another eighteen years. In 1902 she sold it to Montana Senator William Clark for his San Pedro, Los Angeles & Salt Lake Railroad.

Town lots for sale at a two-day public auction, May 15 and 16, 1905, attracted three thousand bidders and spectators who offered prices as high as $1,750 to buy part of William A. Clark's Las Vegas Townsite east of the railroad tracks. On the west side, another Las Vegas was already growing. (Special Collections, UNLV Library)

The Stumbling First Step

In 1902, James T. McWilliams, a half-forgotten civil engineer and surveyor from Canada, carried out a survey of 1,800 acres that Mrs. Helen J. Stewart owned in the Las Vegas Valley. McWilliams discovered that eighty acres adjoining Mrs. Stewart's property were still available and filed a claim. He was one of the first men to see the possibility of a town growing up around the bubbling springs in Southern Nevada.

Rumors had been circulating for years that a railroad would be built between Salt Lake City and the fast-growing California city of Los Angeles, and the Las Vegas Valley was a natural stopover and watering point for a rail line. While the population of the Las Vegas Valley was just nineteen in 1900 and had grown to no more than thirty by early 1904, McWilliams felt certain that a boom was inevitable.

Using his experience as a surveyor, McWilliams laid out his town in 1904 and began selling lots for as little as one hundred dollars each to a varied crowd—miners, railroad workers, cowboys, gamblers, and a sprinkling of professional thieves. Within a few weeks, this first Las Vegas had a hotel, a meat market, a little store, four restaurants, a dozen bars and gambling halls—all built of canvas over wood frames and in danger of being blown away by the desert winds.

But McWilliams faced a threat greater than the unpredictable valley weather: the rivalry of a rich, influential, and notoriously corrupt U.S. senator, William Clark of Montana, founder of the San Pedro, Los Angeles & Salt Lake Railroad.

The Arrival of the Copper King

"I never bought a man who wasn't for sale" is often quoted as the defense offered by William Clark when he was charged with bribery. Whether he was ever quite that candid about his purchase of favors, Clark was widely known for his use of spectacular bribes—sometimes paying off fellow politicians with thousand-dollar bills.

A decade before he decided to build a railroad from Salt Lake City to Los Angeles, and to establish a stopover at a town he planned to call Las Vegas, Clark set out to buy enough members of the Montana legislature to win election to the U.S. Senate. This was the late 1890s, when U.S. senators were chosen by state legislators rather than by popular vote.

Clark had one major rival—another copper king named Marcus Daly, a popular, hearty Irishman who was a partner in the powerful Anaconda mines, while Clark was described by historian Joseph Kinsey Howard as "a tight white starched little man" with few friends but an extraordinary determination to obtain a seat in the Senate.

During the angry contest between Clark and Daly, a state senator displayed four envelopes containing a total of thirty thousand dollars, which he said was intended as bribes to his fellow senators, and accused Clark of "purchasing votes like eggs." In one Montana newspaper, a cartoonist drew a thousand-dollar bill and called it "the kind of bill most frequently introduced in the Montana Legislature."

Senator William A. Clark of Montana, founder of the San Pedro, Los Angeles & Salt Lake Railroad, campaigned aboard his private rail car and was accused of buying votes with thousand-dollar bribes. (Special Collections, UNLV Library)

It took eighteen ballots for the state senate to reach a decision, but Clark was finally elected—a Democrat who had persuaded eleven Republicans to support him.

Although this was a period of wide corruption in the election of senators, some members from other states decided that Clark had been a bit too open in purchasing his seat. After listening to ninety witnesses, a U.S. Senate committee declared Clark's election null and void because of the expenditure of more than a third of a million dollars in bribes and other expenses.

Clark resigned—but did not surrender. He and his backers fooled the Republican governor of Montana into taking a journey to a remote town in California, and while he was out of the state and out of touch, a compliant lieutenant-governor appointed Clark to the Senate seat he'd just been forced to vacate.

Even Clark realized that he had gone too far this time. He announced that he would resign and return to Montana to vindicate himself. To the astonishment of his enemies, he was finally elected to the Senate in 1900, but his days there won him no credit. Ellen Maury Sladen, wife of a Texas congressman, left the most vivid portrait of Senator Clark. He was so thin, she said, that his body "just seems [to be] the handle for his yellow mop of curly hair and whiskers." She had heard Washingtonians remark, "if you took away the whiskers and the scandal there would be nothing left of him."

The Uneven Battle

After McWilliams succeeded in selling lots in his "Original Las Vegas Town Site" on the west side of the railroad tracks, Clark began laying out plans for a town on the east side. Clark's Las Vegas Land and Water Company first offered lots for sale for between one hundred and three hundred dollars an acre, but was soon overwhelmed with more than three thousand offers and decided that the announced prices were too low. Clark and his partners canceled the early agreements and scheduled a public auction for May 15 and 16, 1905.

Las Vegas pioneer Ed Von Tobel Jr. recalled that his father noticed an advertisement in the *Los Angeles Times* offering lots for sale in the new town. "He and a buddy thought, well, what the heck, we got nothing to lose, we'll just sign up for a couple of business lots and set up a little lumber yard. He stayed . . . for the rest of his life."

McWilliams responded by publishing newspaper advertisements for his own eighty-acre plat, promising buyers: "Get in line early, buy now, double your money in 60 days." He also warned them about the dangerous lure of the auction Clark was planning: "Auction sales are never good for the buyers. . . . People get excited at auctions and feel like kicking themselves the next day." He said Clark's company had laid out no streets, no sidewalks, no public improvements, and then promised that his own townsite would make such advances "as soon as the railroad townsite, if not sooner."

Three thousand bidders and spectators showed up for Clark's auction. They had been attracted by the offer of special excursions from Los Angeles (for sixteen dollars, round trip) and Salt Lake City (for twenty dollars, round trip). Those who bought a lot received a refund of their fare.

Bids ranged as high as $1,750 for a few prized lots. Within hours after the two-day auction ended, some of McWilliams's settlers moved across the railroad track, hauling or dragging their crudely built wooden structures or tents.

John F. Cahlan, one of the founders of the *Las Vegas Review-Journal,* observed in his oral history: "The only trouble was that [McWilliams] built it before the railroad line came in. What people were over there, they had their business places built on skids. When the railroad came in, they just moved over onto the east side of town. Only those who couldn't afford to move out lived over there."

Neatly divided into identical blocks of land, the basic design for Clark's townsite remains unchanged today. Bright casinos, hotels, and office buildings long ago replaced the early makeshift shelters, but Fremont, Carson, Bridger, and other original streets remain part of Downtown Las Vegas. (Special Collections, UNLV Library)

John F. Cahlan, one of the founders of the *Las Vegas Review-Journal*, recalled his early days as a reporter: "We had the smallest offices of a newspaper I had ever been in. They gave me a four-legged table that had no drawers in it, no storage space or anything. They did put a typewriter on the desk so I could type my stories, but we had no direct connection with any news service. . . . You had to fill the pages, and it was a 4-page newspaper.

"All our daily news came in what we called a 'pony service.' The pony service was about 250 to 300 words a day over the Union Pacific telegraph. The pony was put in what we called 'cablese.' It would put 2 words together so it wouldn't cost so much on the telegraph—'downplay' for 'play down.' They connected the two words together so it wouldn't make sense. Sometimes it was like reading Arabic. I had to fill in the information."

Cahlan traced the failure of McWilliams's "Original Las Vegas Town Site" to two major problems: "They had no indoor plumbing. There wasn't enough assessed valuation over there so that they could pave the streets. They couldn't do anything." To further handicap McWilliams, the railroad built the tracks so high that it was very difficult for wagons to cross from his townsite on the west to Clark's townsite to the east.

An Experiment in Prohibition

In accepting bids, the railroad company stipulated that no liquor could be sold on any of the premises, with the exception of those built on Block 16. Outside that small area, if anyone in the new town sold liquor, his title to the land would revert to the railroad, the contracts said.

One early resident, John Wisner, who had bought lots on Main and Fremont Streets outside Block 16, built the Overland Hotel and opened a saloon. The railroad decided to enforce its restrictions. Pioche was then the county seat, and the railroad sent an employee named Charles (Pop) Squires to Pioche to testify as a witness against Wisner.

"Pop took the train to Caliente—the branch line was built to Pioche—and he was there five days in the middle of the winter," Squires's daughter recalled decades later. "The company, I believe, won the suit on five counts and Wisner was given the decision on three counts, which never decided anything. Since then, there's been no suit or attempt to enforce the 'no liquor' provision.

"When my father got home, he sent in his expense accounts, which he said he arrived at by deducting the three dollars he had in his pocket when he got home from the seventy-five dollars he had when he started out. In a few days, he got a letter back from the

railroad official C. O. Whittemore, which said, 'Squires, the company does not expect to pay for your poker losses in Pioche.' My father wrote in reply, 'Whittemore, when spending five days in Pioche, poker losses are legitimate expenses. Please send check.'

"And they sent the check."

First to Come, First to Go

Many early arrivals in Las Vegas took one quick look around the dusty little settlement and then took the next train out. Those who gave up quickly included twenty-six men who bought business licenses during the excitement of the auction. Some turned in their licenses without ever opening the doors of their businesses. Others simply had second thoughts about settling there and never returned.

Leon H. Rockwell, one of the earliest settlers, recalled the experience of one of the first travelers to arrive in Las Vegas by car. The elderly man had hired a young driver to take him across the desert, and "the inexperienced driver ran the car off the road." With the Ford mired in the sand, neither the owner nor his chauffeur could figure out a way to get it out.

"I'll pull it out for you," said Rockwell, who was passing in another car.

"I don't want it," the discouraged owner said. "I don't want anything to do with it."

"How much do you want for it?" Rockwell asked.

"Anything," the man said.

Rockwell recalls: "I gave him thirty dollars, something like that—and it was a good, new Ford." The owner "threw in an extra tire or two, a tent, and a lot of other stuff," Rockwell remembered—and said farewell to Las Vegas forever.

The Hardest Years

A major fire (of "suspicious origin") destroyed most of McWilliams's Las Vegas late in 1905.

In August 1906, a second disaster discouraged some other early settlers. Thomas Miller, who started on his first visit to Las Vegas by train from Chicago, recalled: "When we arrived, we were informed that the Meadow Valley Wash had gone on a rampage . . . and the road was washed out between Moapa and Caliente. It was necessary to turn the train around and go back to Barstow, and go in over the Santa Fe. Charles Squires, then the agent for the . . . railroad, visited us and informed us that he could not give us any ice for the train because the ice house had burned up that day too."

Some were discouraged by the sweeping winds. One Las Vegan remembered a real estate dealer who would say when he saw the

"It just happened that when they put in the saloons they also brought in some of the girls," businessman Ed Von Tobel Jr. remembered. "The girls were regulated and they had to go to the city doctor once a week for examinations. . . . We lived on North Third Street and quite often in the night time we could hear rinkadink piano playing."

wind blowing from the south: "Real estate's moving up toward Moapa." Then, when the wind shifted and began blowing from the north, he would observe: "There, it's coming back."

Even with all the problems, things nevertheless seemed to be looking up by 1911. Two railroads—the San Pedro, Los Angeles & Salt Lake and a shorter line, the Las Vegas & Tonopah—provided about 450 fairly good jobs in a town of 1,500. (Clark had built the Las Vegas & Tonopah to supply the new mines in Goldfield, Tonopah, and Rhyolite.) The prospects looked promising enough to lead to a doubling of the population by 1913.

But that early boom ended in 1917, when the Las Vegas & Tonopah Railroad went broke, leaving at least 150 jobless. Four years later, Senator William Clark—who was never a highly regarded boss but at least had shown some selfish personal interest in the future of Las Vegas—sold the San Pedro, Los Angeles & Salt Lake to the Union Pacific Railroad.

"If the old management in Los Angeles had run Las Vegas like a company store, the new management in New York barely knew Las Vegas existed," Deke Castleman observed. "Its employees, immediately dissatisfied, joined a nationwide strike of 400,000 railroad workers in 1922. Locally, some violence erupted between strikers and scabs. When the strike was settled, Union Pacific punitively closed the Las Vegas repair shops, eliminating hundreds more jobs and residents."

"The vindictive Union Pacific replaced the repair shops with smelly stockyards," historian Eugene Moehring observed. The town that had been invented for the convenience of the railroad now seemed abandoned by the railroad.

Even as late as 1929, newly arrived newspaperman John Cahlan took a look around and saw little promise in the isolated desert

"The chances are very strong that Las Vegas could've become a ghost town in the 1920s," historian Hal Rothman said. "Without air conditioning Las Vegas is almost uninhabitable in the summertime. And there were relatively few people here and relatively little reason for anyone else to come here."

"When I came, Fremont Street was the only paved street in town, but it was only paved down the middle," John F. Cahlan said. "You parked on each side of the pavement. It was paved because it was part of the state highway.

"Most of the buildings were shacks. Sears Roebuck and the Mesquite Grocery Store were two-story brick buildings, and there were also two 2-story wooden structures—The First State Bank and the Boulder Club. Everybody used to joke that if the bookends—either the First State or the Boulder Club—were burned down, the little joints in between would collapse and disappear."

"Block Sixteen": In the spring of 1906, this was the place to go for beer and whiskey, to have a bite at the Gem lunch counter or try your luck in a game of chance at the Arizona Club. (Nevada Historical Society)

First State Bank: Railroad workers and farmers who did their banking here could have lunch or an ice-cream treat at the same address. By 1907 they could also pick up their mail or send off a letter from the town's first post office, inside the bank. (Nevada Historical Society)

town—and knew that it was viewed with some contempt by people elsewhere in Nevada: "People in the city of Reno or northern Nevada would have been very happy if Las Vegas had seceded from the state. It was just so isolated that there didn't seem to be any possibility that it would grow. When I came down here first, I thought this was the least likely to succeed of any [in] the United States. I made up my mind that I was going to stay here about a year, then try my luck back in New York or Chicago."

But just ahead was a development that would change the unpromising little town forever . . .

President Herbert Hoover sent the U.S. Secretary of the Interior to Las Vegas to decide whether workers on the Hoover Dam could be housed there. Historian Dennis McBride wrote: "The city fathers . . . said, 'Look, we're going to close down Block 16. We're gonna close up the saloons and the bars because we don't want him to think we're as loose and wide open as we are.'"

Hoover Dam, engineering marvel of the 1930s, harnessed the power of the Colorado River to provide electricity for three states. It also created Lake Mead, now the center of a National Recreation Area covering a million and a half acres. (Bureau of Reclamation, May 3, 1995; photography by Andrew Pernick)

4

GATEWAY TO THE DAM

"It's a miracle!" they said. When residents of the dusty little rail-road town heard about government plans to build the biggest dam in the world in their backyard, they celebrated in the wild Las Vegas style of 1928.

Elbert Edwards was one of the revelers. "They just broke loose with everything they had," the school administrator recalled later. "The volunteer fire department turned out in full force, leading the parade. Bootleg liquor just flowed like water."

President Calvin Coolidge had just signed the Boulder Canyon Project Act that meant salvation for Las Vegas. At Black Canyon, less than thirty miles southeast of town, the government was about to begin its most ambitious engineering project since the Panama Canal. The building of Boulder Dam—later named Hoover Dam—would provide work for thousands of jobless people at a time when the rest of the country was struggling through the worst economic depression in United States history. Grubby little Las Vegas was about to become the center of worldwide attention.

Early resident Leon H. Rockwell said he'd never forget the night everybody in town celebrated the news. "When the bill was passed, that's when the excitement was," he remembered. "Nobody thought it might happen, now or maybe 50 years from now. When the bill was signed, we got the fire truck out, and—my God, everybody that

"There are a thousand and six stories that have been told about the construction of Boulder Dam, some of them true and most of 'em false."
—John F. Cahlan, former managing editor of the *Las Vegas Review-Journal*, Oral History memoir

could hooked on to it! In carts and baby buggies and everything else—just like they was nuts. There was people got lit that never had taken a drink before."

What Was All the Shouting About?

Government engineers had been talking about damming the Colorado River since 1905, the year Las Vegas was founded, when a raging flood swept through farms in the Imperial Valley of California. Millions of dollars' worth of crops were destroyed, along with everything else in the path of the flood. After nearly two years of unrelenting destruction, the river suddenly calmed down to a comparative trickle. Now exhausted farmers struggled to cope with devastating drought. They begged the federal government to do something about this unpredictable menace.

That was a job for the Reclamation Service branch of the Department of the Interior. Established in 1902, the branch would soon become a full-fledged federal bureau. When Reclamation geologists, hydrographers, surveyors, and engineers tackled the problem of harnessing the power of the river, they studied dozens of possible damsites.

By 1919 they had narrowed the list to two locations, Boulder Canyon and Black Canyon, two deep gorges just twenty miles apart. Both looked promising—high enough to support a towering dam and narrow enough to fill with a predictable volume of concrete. The final choice would depend upon the strength and stability of the underlying rock formations, as well as the depth of silt and gravel deposits that would have to be dug up and removed.

Precise measurements were vital. The dam had to be infallible. A single mistake could cause the dam to unleash a wall of water, engulfing downstream towns and crashing through levees in the Imperial Valley. So teams of specialists were sent to the two canyons during 1920 to drill, sift, analyze, and observe.

One preliminary reconnaissance team was led by Arthur Powell Davis, director of the U.S. Reclamation Service, who had supervised the design and construction of a long list of dams, tunnels, and irrigation canals. Earlier, he had served as chief hydrographer for the commission choosing the location of the Panama Canal. With the U.S. Geological Survey he had been a topographer and hydrographer. As a nephew of John Wesley Powell, celebrated nineteenth-century explorer of the Colorado River, Davis had grown up with dreams of harnessing the river's power. His visit to Boulder Canyon in November 1920 convinced him that his team had found the ideal spot for the government's big dam.

Preliminary investigations had revealed a granite foundation at Boulder Canyon, presumed more stable than the volcanic tuff at Black Canyon, so the Reclamation Service ordered a full-scale testing program at Boulder Canyon. Walker Young, a thirty-six-year-old engineer, was selected to head the expedition. In January 1921, Young and a crew of fifty-eight men set up their camp on a flat, rocky beach upstream from the canyon walls they were about to study. For nearly a year, the men lived in twenty-eight canvas tents on the beach while they drilled, mapped, analyzed, and risked their necks in flat-bottomed boats, battling treacherous currents in the river. Furnace-like heat forced them to abandon their camp during the summer.

In the end, the granite foundation proved disappointing—full of unexpected joints, faults, and jumbles. Young and his team concluded that Boulder Canyon was not the ideal place for their monumental dam after all. In late December 1921, they moved downstream to Black Canyon, hoping for better results. Almost as soon as they pitched their tents, the new camp was blown away in a

"The Bureau of Reclamation, the builder of Hoover Dam, is part of the Department of the Interior and one of the principal construction agencies of the Federal government. . . . The Bureau has designed and supervised the construction of the world's five largest dams—Hoover on the Colorado River in Arizona and Nevada, Grand Coulee on the Columbia in Washington, Shasta on the Sacramento and Friant on the San Joaquin in California, and Marshall Ford on the Colorado in Texas."—Foreword to *Construction of Hoover Dam*, a booklet prepared for the Department of the Interior

screaming windstorm. Now the men had to rebuild and restock their camp from the ground up.

Refusing to consider the storm a bad omen, Young and his men started over. During the winter of 1922 they drilled, tested, and collected more rock samples. When they finished their investigations in April 1923, Young was convinced that Black Canyon was a much better location for the dam than Boulder Canyon. Not only did it promise a more stable rock foundation, but the place was also easier to reach, just thirty miles from a railroad station in Las Vegas.

That train station at the end of Fremont Street already had seen arrivals and departures of so many scientists, politicians, and visiting dignitaries that rumors were inevitable. Each new arrival generated more speculation. Something important was about to happen.

What's in a Name?

Meanwhile, before the damsite was selected and approved, Reclamation chief Arthur Davis had sent a report to Congress proposing a dam "at or near Boulder Canyon," based on what he had observed during his preliminary visit. This led to the introduction in 1923 of a bill that would be debated in Congress for nearly five years before it finally passed as the Boulder Canyon Project Act of 1928. By that time, Black Canyon had become the approved site, but the press continued to call the proposed structure "Boulder Dam." The American public, it seemed, had speculated about Boulder Dam too long to be willing to accept another name. Even after the dam was finished in 1935 and officially named for Herbert Hoover, most people still called it Boulder Dam.

Hoover had been an enthusiastic advocate of the dam for years, since his first visits to the area as a young civil engineer. Later, as

Making history with a few pen strokes, these men signed the Boulder Canyon Project Act on December 21, 1928, providing $175 million for construction of a dam. Left to right: Elwood Mead, Commissioner of Reclamation; California Representative Phil Swing and U.S. Senator Hiram Johnson, authors of the bill, on either side of President Calvin Coolidge; Addison T. Smith, chairman of the Committee on Reclamation; and W. B. Matthews, general counsel for the Boulder Dam Association. (Special Collections, UNLV Library)

Secretary of Commerce in the Harding administration, he was instrumental in bringing about an agreement among representatives of the seven states affected by the Colorado River. They wanted to know exactly how much of the river's water each state could claim. Unless they could agree upon a fair division of the water, there would be no dam. Commissioners from Arizona, California, Colorado, Nevada, New Mexico, Utah, and Wyoming attended a series of conferences that ended in disagreement every time.

Secretary Hoover suggested a compromise. Instead of arguing about a state-by-state division of the water, he proposed dividing the Colorado Basin into two parts: upper and lower. The two divisions would share the water proportionally, measuring allotments in acre-feet, and would set aside an unapportioned reserve for Mexico, in case a treaty were signed.

Airborne View: A wooden platform, suspended by cables and chains above the unfinished Hoover Dam in 1934, carried official visitors to the site, including this group, unidentified except for U.S. Senator Key Pittman of Nevada and Mrs. Pittman. At that time, Senator Pittman was chairman of the Senate Foreign Relations Committee. (Nevada Historical Society)

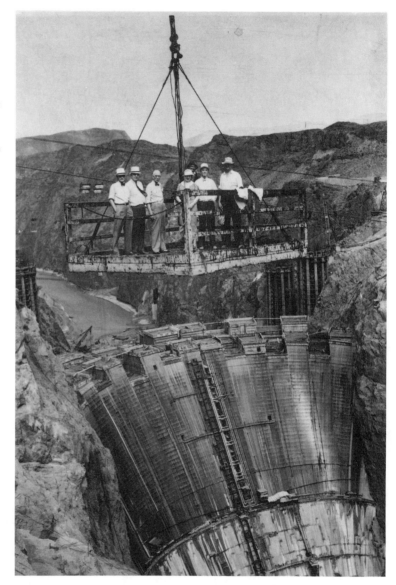

Most of the state commissioners liked the idea. Working together, they hammered out a few details and signed the Colorado River Compact on November 24, 1922. Then they took it back to their state legislatures to be ratified. Arizona was the only dissenter. All the other states adopted the Compact. Finally, after years of legal and scientific disagreement, the Boulder Canyon Project Act of 1928 was signed into law. Two more years would pass before dam construction began in Black Canyon, but Las Vegas didn't wait that long to declare itself the Gateway to the Dam.

Recollections of a River Rat

During the years of congressional debate over the Boulder Canyon Project, self-described "river rat" Murl Emery ran a ferry service on the Colorado River from St. Thomas, a small farming community where his family lived. He had been exploring the Colorado's coves and canyons since boyhood, and he knew the river well. When visiting scientists came out to look at possible sites for the proposed dam, Emery was the expert guide who took them where they wanted to go.

Years later, in oral history interviews, Emery recalled some of his VIP passengers. When General George Washington Goethals, chief engineer for the Panama Canal, came to take a look at the area and offer an opinion, he made a deep impression—but perhaps not the kind of impression the general expected.

"I waited for days for General Goethals to come to show him the damsite and the area," Emery remembered. "When he finally did show up, he showed up with a great big basket of food and big white clean tablecloths. . . . He went outside and laid out his big white tablecloth, brought out his food. All that beautiful food, and he never offered me one stinking bite of it. He kept eating. He would have seen the hungriest ground squirrel in the world if he had just looked up. I didn't like that. He probably didn't like me, either, so we broke even."

Emery had gentler words for the Secretary of Commerce, later President Herbert Hoover. "He was no bother and easy to handle," said the ferry pilot. "By the same token, he was not the kind of a guy you could start up a conversation with."

It was a time when everybody in that part of Nevada speculated about the dam and what it would mean to Las Vegas. All those scientists and engineers who stepped off the train were greeted as evidence that Las Vegas was about to grow into a real city. The new project would provide jobs, money, influence. It didn't matter whether it was called Boulder or Hoover or some other name, the dam would bring the whole world to Las Vegas.

Dam Site Inspectors: Ferry captain Murl Emery (at front of boat) provided the only transportation in 1924 for engineers and financiers who came to the Black Canyon wilderness to look at possible locations for the proposed Hoover Dam. (Photo by N. E. Johnson)

Respectable Las Vegas?

It happened, too, but not quite the way some Las Vegans had imagined the transformation. For a while, they assumed their town would be permanent headquarters for the government project, in spite of the city's lawless reputation.

"Rip-roaring, no-holds-barred pursuit of pleasure was Las Vegas' stock in trade," Joseph E. Stevens wrote in his meticulously researched history, *Hoover Dam: An American Adventure,* "and all that separated it from the frontier towns of the nineteenth century were the automobiles parked in front of the battered hitching posts and the flicker of neon tubes where wooden signboards had once creaked in the wind."

Although the sale of liquor was illegal in the United States at the time, Las Vegas saloons ignored Prohibition laws. Still, Stevens added, "Las Vegas was not all liquor and lights. . . . The town had its small elite of sober, civic-minded citizens who actually thought about the city's future beyond the next Saturday night and strove to give it a veneer of respectability." So, when President Hoover sent his new Secretary of the Interior to see the damsite in the summer of 1929, these sober citizens were determined to make a good impression.

The city fathers ordered all saloons, gambling clubs, and houses of prostitution in Las Vegas to close their doors during the Secretary's visit. No liquor could be sold until the official visitor had left Nevada. When Secretary Lyman Wilbur arrived, accompanied by Elwood Mead, Commissioner of the Bureau of Reclamation, the two dignitaries were given a sedate tour of the city and were escorted back to their railroad car.

The deception might have worked—if some local newspaper reporters hadn't taken an adventurous member of the Wilbur party behind the scenes to the notorious Arizona Club on North First Street. After a few drinks, the errant visitor hurried off to the train and told the Secretary he had found Las Vegas a very hospitable town. Wilbur sniffed the alcoholic fumes and was not amused. Besides, Las Vegas seemed too far away from the damsite for 5,000 workers to commute every day.

Less than two years later, the Bureau of Reclamation announced that the Boulder Canyon Project was going to house its workers in a model town closer to the dam than Las Vegas. Boulder City, a wholesome American community, would be built on federal land.

On May 26, 1931, Nevada Governor Fred Balzar's office in Carson City received a plat and description of the Boulder Canyon Project Federal Reservation. It would cover 144 square miles and would include the damsite, the future Boulder City, and a lot of open territory around the town. Federal jurisdiction was formally established. On the reservation there would be no liquor, no gambling or "other practices deemed injurious to the workers."

Promised Land for the Jobless

Long before the Boulder City plans were announced, Las Vegas was already overflowing with job-seekers. By 1930, thousands of Americans in every state were out of work and hungry. The Great Depression affected everybody. In the East, former executives rubbed elbows with bricklayers in emergency bread lines and soup kitchens. When they heard the news that some fifty million dollars of government money was about to be funneled through Las Vegas to build a dam, anybody who could find a map started looking for a way to get to the Promised Land.

In his Hoover Dam history, Joseph Stevens describes the invasion of Las Vegas:

> Since announcement of the construction timetable in 1930, hundreds of jobless men had been streaming into southern Nevada in caravans of wheezing automobiles, in Union Pacific boxcars, on horseback, and even on foot, coming in a wave the likes of which the state had not seen since the heyday of the Comstock Lode. . . . Most of the newcomers were green-horns—unemployed factory workers, mechanics, salesmen, store clerks, lawyers, bankers and students—who had never performed hard physical labor or lived outdoors. Many of them had brought their families and household belongings, gambling everything that at Hoover Dam they would find jobs

and a new beginning. But the work had not yet begun, and instead of a new beginning the migrants encountered the same problems and hardships they were trying to escape.

Years later, people who were there in the 1920s and 1930s remembered what it was like when "the whole world" began to arrive, looking for jobs. They told their stories in oral histories preserved in collections at the University of Nevada in Reno and Las Vegas and in the Boulder City library.

Las Vegas newspaperman John F. Cahlan was there when the builders—Six Companies, Incorporated, of San Francisco—won the contract for $48,890,000, the largest labor contract awarded by the United States government up to that time. He remembered the chaos: "If you haven't lived through it, you can't imagine what would happen to a little railroad community of 5,000 people having 10,000 to 20,000 people dumped on it all at one time. There wasn't any money available. You had to provide schools for the kids. You had to provide facilities for the community. We just didn't know what to do."

"Everybody was coming," George L. Ullom recalled. "They were living under the bushes. . . . There'd be two hundred people sleeping either on the ground or on the benches."

Cahlan remembered the long lines of hopeful job applicants outside the employment office: "During the early part of the summer of the year the contract was let, the United States government put up an employment building in Las Vegas; it was across the street from the present county courthouse. It was just a one-room shack . . . and all hiring had to come through that one building. . . . For many months you would have lines of men a block or a block-and-a-half long, waiting to get in for applications for employment. . . . And during the construction . . . we would have Ph.D.s

The *Las Vegas Evening Review and Journal,* January 1, 1931, displayed this front-page headline:

OPEN BOULDER DAM BIDS
MARCH 4 TO BE FINISHED
MAY 15, 1938

The dam was completed more than two years ahead of schedule and was dedicated on September 30, 1935, by President Franklin D. Roosevelt. The first generator began producing power on October 22, 1936. Before the end of that year, two more generators were in operation.

working on a muck stick, in the mines, or in the tunnel down there, and people that used to be on Wall Street driving trucks."

Crowds were so thick around the employment office that casual strollers had to find another route. When reporter Thomas Wilson arrived to take a job on the *Las Vegas Age,* he saw the crowds and asked, "Is there going to be a parade or something?" He was told, "Oh, those are men waiting for jobs on the dam." Each applicant had a story to tell:

Joe Kine was out of a job in 1931 when the Oklahoma mine where he worked closed down. "I picked strawberries to make a little money. I tried selling Real Silk Hosiery and a few things like that. But I heard about this going on out here, so I bought a Model T Ford for $10 and drove it out. . . . I sold my Model T Ford after I got here, for $2.50. I wish I had it back now."

Harry Hall was in the same boat. "Nevada was the only place you could get a job," he recalled. "Jobs were very hard to come by, so we decided to come out here and try our luck."

Tommy Nelson, a nineteen-year-old trumpet player, needed a steady job. "I was just a dumb kid from Ely," he said later. "Things were pretty rough, but my father had a job down here, so I came, too." Nelson's father, who ran the commissary at the construction site, got Tommy a job as a laborer, but the young musician kept on playing the trumpet in his spare time and eventually became part of the entertainment scene in Las Vegas.

Treasuring the Memories

Kine, Hall, and Nelson were just three of the thousands of men who came from every part of America to work on the dam. Some stayed long after the dam was completed, settling down in Boulder City and Las Vegas to raise their families. Others moved away but never

"As you walk along Denver Street, you can see two prominent houses on the hilltop west of the watertank. The largest was the Executive Lodge for Six Companies, Inc., the general contractor for the dam. The large ten room house was used by the executives of Six Companies and other dignitaries including President Herbert Hoover when visiting the Project site."—*Boulder City Historic District Walking Tours,* brochure published by the City of Boulder City

Taps at the Dam: Tommy Nelson, a charter member of the Musicans Union, Las Vegas Local 369, never misses a reunion of the 31ers Club— those who worked on the Hoover Dam between 1931 and 1936. In those days he played his trumpet nightly in a dance band at Railroad Pass, a small nightclub three miles outside of strait-laced Boulder City, after working all day as a laborer. Now, more than sixty years later, he plays taps every Memorial Day for comrades who have died since the last gathering of 31ers. (Glen Marullo)

forgot those years of makeshift living, backbreaking labor, and camaraderie. Twenty years after the job ended, their nostalgia led to the organization of The 31ers Club, those who worked on the Hoover Dam between 1931 and 1936.

Every year since 1956 these survivors have met in Boulder City to celebrate, look at scrapbooks, and exchange memories of the time when they were building the biggest dam in the world. Not many are left now. At the 1996 reunion of The 31ers Club, Tommy Nelson played taps for those who had died since the last gathering. Each Memorial Day, he plays taps at the Boulder City cemetery.

Only eight surviving workers turned up for the 1995 reunion, but they were surrounded by new members. By that time, membership had been expanded to include descendants of 31ers and anyone who had lived in Boulder City for at least thirty-one years.

Among the newer members is Pat Lappin, curator of the Boulder City Hoover Dam Museum, who moved to Boulder City as a teenager in 1941 and was a member of the first graduating class of Boulder City High School. Lappin estimates that there may be as few as 100 survivors of the approximately 5,000 workers who built the dam. "Most of those still alive are in their eighties and nineties now and are just too old to travel."

One of the youngest 31ers is Nevada author Dennis McBride, a Boulder City native, born there in 1955. Fascinated by his hometown's history, he established the Boulder City Library Oral History Project in 1985 with a grant from the Nevada Humanities Committee and started recording reminiscences of dam workers and early Boulder City residents. McBride quoted some of these stories in articles for the *Las Vegas Sun* and in books about Boulder City.

"I grew up hearing stories about the building of the dam," he said, "so it was natural that I would want to write about it." During five years as a special collections librarian at UNLV, McBride discovered more recorded treasures and continued to write about his favorite subject. With the 1993 publication of *Building Hoover Dam: An Oral History of the Great Depression,* McBride and his co-author, Andrew J. Dunar, presented individual stories from many oral history sources woven into a dramatic history told by those who lived it.

Laborers and bosses, homemakers and engineers, storekeepers and newspaper reporters recreate details of the jobs they did, people they remember, and everyday life in a model town. Almost every one of them has something to say about Sims Ely, Boulder City's autocratic manager. Appointed by Secretary Lyman Wilbur to run this government town, Ely was the austere, unsmiling, absolute ruler of the whole reservation.

Dictator of Boulder City

"They used to speak of him during dam construction days as 'the Hitler of Boulder City,'" Elbert Edwards recalled. "He had the assignment by the government to keep the town clean. When a foreman showed up in town drunk, that foreman was exiled from the community."

"Ely was a very, very hard man," said John Cahlan. "He was hard to interview; he wouldn't talk very much. He sat up there on the throne. You couldn't get much out of him. Sims Ely was a virtual czar. . . . There was nothing that went on that he didn't handle. He had tunnel vision. If you didn't believe the way he believed, you didn't live there."

"There is an enduring strangeness at the Boulder Dam Hotel in Boulder City, Nevada. Reality slips beyond reach there like a cat along the corridors, and the cool whispers of what's gone before tickle your ear. . . . The characters who drift in and out of the hotel's history still drift in and out of its rooms and the dark echo of these drifting shadows has given the Boulder Dam Hotel a voice and a life of its own."
—Dennis McBride, *Midnight on Arizona Street: The Secret Life of the Boulder Dam Hotel*

Ragtown provided crude shelter in the 1930s for families who migrated to Nevada hoping to leave the Great Depression behind when they found jobs on the Boulder Dam Project. (Nevada Historical Society)

"He was a dictator in the city," said Carl Merrill. "He made the rules. If you broke the rules, you went up before Sims Ely."

Mary Ann Merrill agreed. "He was a hard man. I guess he was fair in a lot of ways, but he had his own ideas and he put them into practice. And you had to go by his rules. He thought of it as his town. I've heard it said so many times: 'This is Sims's town.'"

"It's hard to imagine one man with this much power over American citizens," Dennis McBride wrote, "but Boulder City was a fenced-in autocracy and the city manager was the dictator."

Dislike for Sims Ely seems to have been nearly universal, but most people agreed that Ely didn't especially want to be liked. "Respect, not affection, was his goal," Joseph Stevens wrote, "and power, not persuasion, his means of achieving it. He would be critical, cantankerous and crotchety, and he would always be right."

Ely's strict ordinances prohibiting alcohol and gambling were acceptable to families who felt safe and comfortable in a town where everything was regulated. But single workers who lived in regimented dormitories found these rules oppressive. On weekends, after days of backbreaking labor in the blazing heat of Black Canyon, these men left the government compound and hurried to Las Vegas where gambling was legal and small night clubs promised a little gaiety. Even if they emptied their pockets at the tables, they seemed willing to keep coming back to the bright lights of Fremont Street. They returned to their dormitories with caution, knowing that if they were found drunk, Sims Ely's judgment would be harsh.

Some Las Vegans give Ely a lot of credit for building their city's reputation as a wide-open Wild West town, a place to "cut loose." They watched Las Vegas grow as the dam progressed and Boulder City remained quiet and orderly. Fremont Street was busier than

At the Movies: In the 1930s, Boulder City's theater was showing *Scarface,* the latest Howard Hughes production, with a Laurel and Hardy comedy and a newsreel. (Special Collections, UNLV Library)

ever, and Las Vegas promoters capitalized on the slogan "Gateway to the Dam."

Twentieth-Century Marvel

By 10:30 A.M. on September 30, 1935, traffic on the new Nevada Highway between Las Vegas and Boulder City was nearly bumper to bumper. President Franklin Delano Roosevelt was riding in an open touring car, waving to crowds along the road, on his way to dedicate the brand-new dam. Inside the federal reservation, thousands of onlookers had gathered to cheer the president, the engineers, the workers, and their massive creation. Except for a few finishing touches, the dam was completed.

At the dedication site, schoolgirls in starched dresses and boys

President Franklin D. Roosevelt dedicated Boulder Dam on September 30, 1935, calling it "a twentieth century marvel" as the nation tuned in on millions of radio sets. (Nevada Historical Society)

with slicked-down hair followed their parents through the crowd, looking for places to stand with an unblocked view of the speakers' platform. Some seized the chance to show off what they had learned about the dam in school and in the pages of *My Weekly Reader:* The highest dam in the world! Seven million tons of concrete—enough to pave a two-lane highway from Miami to Los Angeles, or a five-foot walkway between the North and South Poles. The spillways are big enough to float a battleship. Each intake tower is as high as a thirty-four-story building. A thousand miles of steel pipe and eighteen million pounds of construction steel are somewhere inside this concrete wonder.

When they looked across the lip of the dam, spectators could see the sparkling waters of a lake that hadn't been there before, miraculously rising. When they turned their attention to the red-white-and-blue-draped platform, they saw dignitaries from Washington, D.C., and six state governments waiting to greet the president. As Roosevelt took his seat, smiling and waving at the crowd, Interior Secretary Harold Ickes stepped to the microphone to deliver the first speech. Boulder Dam, Ickes said, would produce wealth to benefit generations of Americans.

In other parts of the country, thousands of people turned on their radios to hear the president's address. For them, after five years of depression, the dam had become a symbol of the optimism and prosperity promised by Roosevelt's New Deal. The president's comforting patrician voice was familiar to millions through his frequent radio talks, and when he began to speak, the crowd strained forward to hear it all. "Ten years ago," he said, "the place where we are gathered was an unpeopled, forbidding desert. . . . The site of Boulder City was a cactus-covered waste. The transformation wrought here is a twentieth century marvel."

He christened that marvel "Boulder Dam." Although an act of

"Morry M. Senoff . . . had bought the *Boulder City News* on July 1, 1948. In 1950 its flag was proclaiming Boulder City as the 'HOME OF HOOVER DAM' and 'The Oasis of the Desert.' Above the nameplate it ran a montage photograph two inches deep across the top of the page. The photos, showing views of the dam and rafting on the Colorado River, were captioned: 'IN BEAUTIFUL BOULDER CITY' and 'THE RECREATION CENTER OF THE SOUTHWEST'."—Jake Highton, *Nevada Newspaper Days*

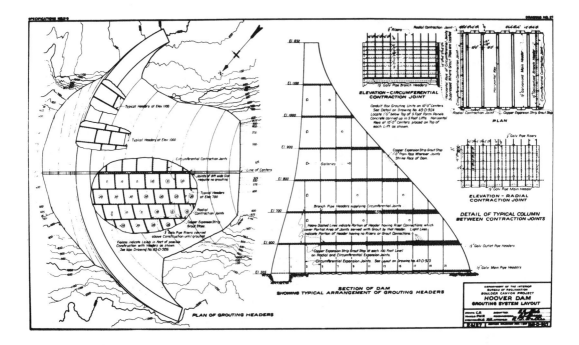

Planning Stage: As early as 1930, Hoover Dam engineers were consulting volumes of diagrams, such as this layout for a grouting system. (Nevada Historical Society)

Congress had named it Hoover Dam when construction began in 1930, the original name was still in common use. Most people continued to call it "Boulder" until 1947, when President Harry Truman recalled the earlier congressional act and suggested that Hoover's name be restored. Once again, Congress acted and Boulder Dam became Hoover Dam.

After the dedication, there was still work to be done. More than 500 laborers stayed in Black Canyon to finish details and mop up the construction site. In February 1936 the Bureau of Reclamation named the reservoir behind the dam Lake Mead, honoring Commissioner Elwood Mead who had died a week earlier. On March 1, Secretary Ickes formally accepted the dam and power house from

Six Companies, Inc. The contractors had finished the job in five years—exactly two years, one month, and twenty-eight days ahead of schedule.

Boulder City has its own quirky history. For a while, there were rumors that the town would simply close down when the dam project ended, but comfortable families were reluctant to move. Over the years, the government found other uses for the reservation. As Boulder City grew during World War II, so did the costs of running the town. After the war, the Bureau of Reclamation was ready to set it free, but Boulderites protested loudly.

"Boulder City was a delightful place to live," said longtime resident Alice Hamilton. "We were well protected and it was a beautiful little city under government control. Most of the old timers liked it that way."

Until 1960 Boulder City was still owned and run by the U.S. Bureau of Reclamation. Since then, it has become an independent municipality where residents own their homes and small businesses. Many people commute every day to jobs in Las Vegas.

In 1983 Boulder City was named a National Historic District. Bars and liquor stores are legal now, but gambling is still forbidden. You won't find any casinos in Boulder City.

"I believed in our town, in its law and order, in its protected place in the bosom of the government's care; I even believed in the government's right to design a concrete structure to stop the flow of a mighty river and create order for the earth. I believed in everything because I needed to be unified with my family. . . .

"If I had to stop time, I'd stop it right there where we were united in our certainty. . . . I'd stop time right at that moment, before the test jets from Nellis Air Force Base began splitting the sky every day with a sonic boom, before the test sites and the atom bomb clouds that flowered on the early morning horizon, too big for me to comprehend."—Phyllis Barber, *How I Got Cultured*

Evolution of Fremont Street: On the first paved street in Las Vegas, the first hotels and banks, first movie theater, first casinos and neon signs reflected the city's growth. Wartime prosperity in the 1940s brought traffic jams. By 1998 the "Fremont Street Experience" was a nightly animated show. (Nevada Historical Society)

5

POLITICS, LAS VEGAS STYLE

"The Only Law in Town"

Harvey Hardy, a young mining engineer, discovered how tough the newly founded town of Las Vegas was when he and a friend went there to celebrate Christmas Day in 1905. Hardy usually left his savings on deposit at the general store in Goodsprings, Nevada, and when he went in to take out fifty dollars for his trip, the owner, a man named Sam, asked, "What are you going to do with it?"

"I'm heading for Las Vegas," Hardy told him.

Sam reacted immediately by asking, "Have you got a gun?"

Hardy said he had one, but he'd left it up at the mine, which was some distance from Goodsprings.

Sam told him to wait, then went back into his living quarters and returned after a couple of minutes with a .38 Smith and Wesson "with pearl handles and a bright shiny nickel plated frame."

"Now put that in your belt and be damned careful," Sam told Hardy. "That's a tough town over there and they tell me they get a man for breakfast pretty near every morning."

After putting the gun in his belt, Hardy joined a friend named Harry for an eight-mile walk to Jean, where they caught the train to Las Vegas. When they arrived, Hardy and his friend decided to spend the night at what someone had told them was the best hotel in town. It "was really a big tent with a wood floor and canvas hung

Big Fellow: Sam Gay enforced law and order in rowdy Las Vegas with a six-shooter, even before he was elected county sheriff. (Special Collections, UNLV Library)

up to divide the spaces," Hardy recalled seven decades later. It was fancier than other hurriedly erected hotels because guests were provided with a double bed, a wash-basin, and a pitcher of water.

After dropping by the town's first church, Hardy and his friend Harry went to "the only place that offered any alternate form of entertainment." This was the notorious Block 16 — the block the railroad had set aside for bars and gambling, and which had already become the town's lively redlight district.

("One of the most active trades was for ladies of easy virtue, who moved in and were well established before [the town] hardly got started," one early Las Vegas resident remembered.)

"Along about midnight in one of the joints," Hardy recalled, "while Harry was trying to solve the mysteries of roulette and I was having a drink with a couple of newfound friends, a big fellow tapped me on the shoulder and said, 'Come on over here out of this crowd. I want to talk to you.'"

After leading the puzzled Hardy to a quieter spot, the "big fellow" said: "You boys seem to be strangers here. Where do you come from?" Hardy told him.

"The reason I'm talking to you like this is because I am the night watchman in this town and the only law here," the man said. "I don't want to see any trouble so I am going to give you some advice. There are a dozen fellows here who have seen you boys spend a little money and they have been following you around. Any one of them would be glad of a chance to knock you in the head for a dollar. So when you go home stay in the middle of the road all the time and don't go near any bushes."

After midnight, Hardy and Harry started back to their hotel.

"Across the street from Block 16 was a vacant block with a wagon road angling across it to our hotel," Hardy recalled. He and Harry decided to take this short-cut, forgetting the advice offered by the "big fellow."

"About the middle of the block the road passed between two mesquite bushes," Hardy remembered. "When we were almost up to the bushes a man stepped out from each of them and advanced towards us in a very unfriendly manner." Hardy suddenly recalled that he had Sam's gun in his pocket. He pulled it out. Noticing the moonlight reflected by the nickel plating, "Our two friends faded back into the bushes."

Verdicts Without Trials

Harvey Hardy learned later that the "big fellow" who had suggested that he watch his step in Las Vegas was Sam Gay.

"I guess Sam was 6'6" one way, and 6'4" the other," one early settler recalled. "He had a hand that was 12 inches by 12, anyway. I know I have seen him handle a .44 six-shooter, and he seemed to just palm that .44 with its six-inch barrel."

Gay, after first volunteering to keep order in the lawless little town, was later elected county sheriff. He was noted for rounding up men he thought were likely to cause trouble, marching them to the edge of town, and encouraging them to keep going.

One early settler, Leon H. Rockwell, recalls seeing Gay coming along one afternoon with his "parade."

"There was sixteen of them," Rockwell recalls, "two abreast, and he was in back of them. They started pretty fast, because he kicked . . . one . . . with the bottom of his foot, and just lifted him right off the ground." Rockwell watched the men hurrying ahead of Gay. "You could just see a string of dust," he said. Later Rockwell said to Gay, "Well, Sam, you sure got rid of them easy."

"You know," Gay replied, "that saved the state and county a lot of money. If I'd taken them to court, all they'd have done was give them a short sentence. We'd have had to ship them up, we'd have fed them until they got the wrinkles out of their bellies, and then they'd turn them loose. Now, these men will never come back as long as I'm here."

"And," Rockwell commented, "they never did."

One Way to Set a Fine

Rockwell recalled a justice of the peace named Jacob Ralph and a cooperative deputy sheriff who worked out an equally simple way of dealing with suspected crimes without wasting a lot of time on trials. Judge Ralph was also a blacksmith and used his shop on First Street as a courtroom.

"In his shop there was a tub that he kept full of water in which to temper his irons," one early settler remembered. "The overflow formed a muddy pool in the dirt floor in which his white Pekin ducks delighted to waddle and quack. While the judge was holding court it was difficult to distinguish the voices of the witnesses from the voices of the ducks."

The testimony of the witnesses didn't always matter very much to Judge Ralph anyway, Rockwell said. The collaborating deputy sheriff would arrest a stranger and bring him into Ralph's court. The judge had one important preliminary question to ask about the stranger. "How much does he have in his pocket?" he would whisper to the deputy sheriff.

Whatever that total turned out to be, the judge would fine the stranger that amount, and later the deputy and the judge would split the fine fifty-fifty.

Gold from the North

One early settler recalls that political bosses from the distant, powerful city of Reno would make visits to the dusty little town to the south whenever an election for the state legislature was scheduled, since controlling legislators could be profitable.

When they came south, the politicians brought sacks of gold pieces with them. When they arrived in Las Vegas, they would begin by dropping by Block 16. There they would invite a group of the most attractive and popular girls to accompany them on their mission. The visitors and the girls would then make the rounds of the town's many saloons, and word would circulate quickly that rewards were waiting for anyone who was ready to carry out his civic duty by voting for the right candidate.

By the time gambling was legalized in 1931, many Nevadans had formed a deep suspicion of all politicians.

"The men who ran the casinos fully understood politics probably better than anyone, since they had been paying off politicians for years and years and years," says Nicholas Pileggi, author of *Casino.*

Las Vegans' prevailing doubts about the honesty of political leaders were increased by two episodes during the 1930s and early 1940s.

William Moore, one of the first members of the Nevada Tax Commission, recalled what it was like in Nevada before the commission was set up to control gambling. Anyone could go to a sheriff or the city commission and say, "I'm going to build a gambling casino, and I'm going to need a license," Moore said, and in many parts of the state, the sheriff would respond: "Well, when I have certain monies cross my hands, why, you'll have the license."

The Mystery of the Missing Mayor

By the early 1930s, many people in Las Vegas were angry with Ed Clark, the most powerful banker in town, who also controlled the power, water, and telephone companies.

Some Las Vegans complained of finding tadpoles in the water when they turned on the taps. Others referred to the town's power lines as "Ed Clark's clothesline."

Bill German, an early city commissioner, voted against a proposal to put the city's electrical wires underground. He explained his reason: "The first time we have a rainstorm, the whole community will be shocked."

"That name was hung on the power company because every time it rained, the lights went out," editor John Cahlan recalled in his oral history. Even between rains there was a problem: "You didn't have any electricity during the daytime, because they generated it with a big generator they called 'Big Betsy,'" Cahlan recalled. "Since the single overused generator was frequently out of operation for hours, you had to listen for the sound of Big Betsy running, and then you could turn on your lights and get power."

"The power company only ran in the night, and the telephone company only in the daytime," another early Las Vegan recalled.

Power Man: Controversial banker Ed Clark controlled the city's telephone service, water, and electrical power in the 1930s. (Special Collections, UNLV Library)

News Man: John F. Cahlan reported Las Vegas political battles for the *Review-Journal*. (Special Collections, UNLV Library)

During the ten years Ernie Cragin was mayor, people grumbled but no action was taken. Cragin himself, a very popular figure, was well satisfied with the way things were going. In addition to enjoying the exercise of great political power, he was a partner in the town's two theaters and co-owner of an insurance business. During his spare time he refereed prize fights.

But by the middle of the 1930s things began to change. A man named Leonard Arnett arrived in Las Vegas, and he was considerably more vocal about the tadpoles in the water supply and more critical about the tendency of lights to go out unexpectedly than most citizens. He soon found an ally named John L. (Johnny) Russell, and together they stirred up strong support for a radical idea—city ownership of the utilities. In 1935 Arnett ran for mayor on a platform calling for public ownership of the power company.

"Municipal power split the town," said Cahlan of the *Review-Journal.* "Pop" Squires, editor of the competing newspaper, the *Age,* "took the attitude that municipal power would be a solution to all the problems we had—not only municipal power but municipal utilities."

Arnett, with the support of labor unions and the *Age,* helped introduce a referendum to allow voters to express their views on municipally owned utilities—and the vote was overwhelming: 2,117 in favor of the city taking over water and power services, and only 215 against.

With an almost ten-to-one victory, and the election of a new mayor, the days of Ed Clark's primitive utility services seemed to be numbered. But then the great crusade ran into some unanticipated problems. Ed Clark's attorneys challenged the proposed changeover in court, and while a complicated legal battle was still shaping up, newly elected mayor Arnett made a surprising request.

"The few doctors who were here never performed any operation unless it was an emergency," John F. Cahlan recalled about early Las Vegas. "They would ship their patients to Los Angeles or to Salt Lake City for any ordinary operation. If they did operate here, they'd set the operation for 3 or 4 in the morning and line the operating room with ice, so it would be cool enough. . . ." There was no chiropodist in town. "One man used to make the circuit of all the small towns around this area. He'd come about once a month or every two months, and everybody would line up to get their feet fixed." Cahlan remembered going to the same doctor for the delivery of his daughter and for treatment for a sick collie.

Charlie (Pop) Squires, proprietor of one of the first Las Vegas hotels and founder of the *Las Vegas Age,* had great influence in early Las Vegas, even though most of his businesses failed. His daughter recalled one of the reasons: "During the Depression, several old prospectors would come in every few weeks and say, 'Charlie, can you let me have a little money to eat on?' And Pop would give them a five-dollar bill. Finally I said to him, 'Pop, you can't afford to do that.' I've never forgotten his reply. He said, 'Sister, I can't afford not to. I know I'm going to have a good dinner and a comfortable bed, and I'd never be able to close my eyes if I thought those poor devils didn't have something to eat or a place to lay their heads.'"

He asked that he be given a sixty-day leave of absence because of a vague health problem. The city council approved this odd request, and then Arnett mysteriously disappeared.

"He left here practically overnight and went to Petaluma, where, I am told, he bought a rather large chicken ranch," Cahlan recalled. "As far as the people who knew him knew, he did not have that kind of money that would purchase a lot of land in California. There was a rumor around town that he was bought off. I don't want to get into that area because it was nothing but a rumor. Nobody knew whether it was Ed Clark, whether it was Ernie Cragin or who it was.

"I tried to put two and two together: here is a man who was for municipal power, and the powers that be were against municipal power, and Arnett left here without telling anybody. I guess he told his wife and daughter, but nobody knew that he was going to leave. He sent a telegram from Petaluma as his resignation. As anybody would do, we tried to put two and two together, and came up with the answer. The answer we figured was that he was bought off."

The Tangled Web

In 1939 Johnny Russell, who, like the disappearing Arnett, advocated municipal ownership of the utilities, was chosen as mayor. The town's four city commissioners blocked his program, and after some months of bickering, all four of them resigned, leaving the mayor the town's only elected officer.

A group of prominent business leaders met and voted to replace the elected commissioners with four men they had chosen. Then the city attorney made a decision. The four elected commissioners couldn't just resign, he said. They would have to schedule a formal meeting where they, as commissioners, would have to vote to accept their own resignations. The four considered the attorney's order, then changed their minds and decided to remain in office.

But Mayor Russell, who had been disappointed by the behavior of the elected commissioners, formally appointed the four new commissioners who had been chosen by the civic leaders. The city now had two boards of commissioners.

All this was happening at the time the U.S. Army had decided to establish an aerial gunnery school at the Las Vegas airport. The Army needed the approval of the Las Vegas city government, and a decision was urgent. Both sets of commissioners met simultaneously to consider this important proposal. Mayor Russell met with the group of newly appointed commissioners around the board table in city hall. The elected commissioners met at the other end of the room, with one of them acting as mayor.

The city clerk, trying desperately to keep everything legal, moved back and forth from one part of the room to the other, spending a few minutes alternately with each group.

Democrats dominated Las Vegas politics for many years. "No Republican was important, as far as Las Vegas was concerned," John F. Cahlan recalled. "Even the Republican state committee would say that we can hold our convention in a phone booth." The most influential political leader was Ed W. Clark, who dominated the Las Vegas economy in the 1930s. "As his was the only bank in town, he could, if he so desired, control the politics, because there were a lot of high-powered politicians who had loans in the bank. Ed usually chose those he wanted as members of the city commission and the county commission."

Charges Against the Mayor

Soon after that strange double session, one of the original elected commissioners filed charges against Mayor Russell, and a court ruled that Russell had to appear before the old board (which he had replaced) to defend himself against the accusations.

The old board heard the mayor, then voted to remove him from office. But before the new legal tangle could be worked out, the besieged mayor died after a heart attack.

Both boards finally realized that no satisfactory solution to the complicated situation was possible. The old elected board dis-

Seeking a Master Plan:
In the 1970s, city leaders invited representatives of sixty Las Vegas professional and philanthropic organizations to recommend plans for the city's future. At a joint conference, Nevada artist Caral Lee Conte, representing the League of Women Voters, made these sketches of (clockwise from the top) Mayor Oran Gragson and Commissioners Hal Morelli, George D. Franklin, Alexander Coblenz, and Hank Thornley. (Caral Lee Conte)

solved itself. The temporary mayor who headed the city government after Russell's conviction resigned, and the other unelected commissioners surrendered their offices. A new mayor and four new commissioners were elected, all promising fervently to restore civic harmony.

A calmer period in Las Vegas politics had begun, but the question of the future development of the town was being settled far from the municipal offices, out on a dusty highway.

Trailblazer: Three miles south of Las Vegas, visionary hotelman Tom Hull built the El Rancho Vegas and was criticized for choosing a site so remote. But his successful hotel-casino set the stage for a string of later resorts that became the Las Vegas Strip. (Special Collections, UNLV Library)

6

INVENTING THE STRIP

The Beginning of the Strip

One widely accepted legend traces the origin of the Las Vegas Strip back to an afternoon in 1941 when Los Angeles hotelman Tom Hull had a flat tire on the narrow road leading to Los Angeles. While waiting for somebody to come out to fix the tire, the legend says, Hull noticed how many automobiles were passing the site, and this gave him an idea.

"He decided that he would build a hotel [there] to take advantage of the tourist travel," John F. Cahlan, editor of the *Las Vegas Review-Journal,* said later. "Then some local people suggested that to take advantage of legalized gambling, he should build a gambling casino with motel rooms around it."

In *Resort City in the Sunbelt,* Eugene P. Moehring reports that Hull's decision to build his motel-casino on what became the Strip was less accidental. Moehring credits two Las Vegas businessmen, Robert Griffith and James Cashman, with inviting Hull to Las Vegas in early 1940 and convincing him that he should build his next resort in Southern Nevada.

Whatever persuaded him, Hull decided to build the first casino on a stretch of desert land three miles from the center of Las Vegas, and to call it the El Rancho—a name he had previously used for hotels in Indio, Sacramento, and Fresno, California.

In 1931 Freshman Assembly-
man Phil Tobin of Humboldt
County introduced the bill that
legalized gambling in Nevada.
He later told Tim Anderson of
the *Reno Gazette-Journal* his
reasons for favoring repeal of
the antigambling laws: "I was
just plumb sick and tired of
seeing gambling going on all
over the state and payoffs being made everywhere. Some
of those tinhorn cops were col-
lecting 50 bucks a month for
allowing it. Also, the damn
state was broke and we
needed the money."

Hull began by buying thirty-three acres for $150 an acre—from a woman who was astonished at the generosity of his offer, since she thought the dusty land was worthless. (Earlier, John Cahlan reported, property along the highway to Los Angeles "could've been bought for twenty-five dollars an acre—or for taxes.")

A neon windmill on the roof of his casino attracted the attention of drivers en route to Las Vegas from California. In addition to his well-designed western motel, Hull offered guests a swimming pool and horseback riding trails, some small shops, and a travel agency.

"The casino was small," Robert D. McCracken writes in *Las Vegas: The Great American Playground.* "It had only one craps table, two blackjack tables, and one roulette wheel." He adds: "El Rancho Vegas also offered entertainment, including a chorus line of scantily clad girls with good figures (plump, by today's standards), brought in from Hollywood. Big names, including Milton Berle, Jackie Gleason, Jimmy Durante, and later Dean Martin, Jerry Lewis [and] Sammy Davis, Jr. . . . were used to attract and hold crowds and high rollers."

Las Vegans applauded Hull's readiness to take the risk in building the El Rancho, but most of them felt certain his investment was doomed because the casino was too far out of town. The city limits ended then at Fifth Street, and there was nothing but vacant land between the town limits and the El Rancho. The doubters were startled when his motel-casino not only survived but was expanded—finally offering a total of 220 rooms.

The New Frontier

R. E. Griffith, who owned a chain of 475 movie theaters in four southwestern states, took a business trip west in 1941. He was planning to start a national chain of hotels and considered building the first one in Deming, New Mexico. But after examining the town, he decided Deming had as many hotels as it could support.

He continued his journey west, and when he reached Las Vegas he found a much more promising possibility. He saw that Tom Hull's El Rancho was prospering and decided to build a second motel and casino two miles farther from downtown Las Vegas.

The price of land had increased a bit since Hull's $150-an-acre bargain, but owners were still astonished by the fact that anyone wanted to buy land so far out of town.

Griffith approached Guy McAfee, a former Los Angeles vice squad captain who had discovered that more money was to be made from promoting vice than from trying to stamp it out. McAfee was operating a small club called the Pair-O-Dice out on the gravel road leading to Los Angeles, but was ready to sell out—for a price.

The Texas tycoon considered McAfee's thirty-five acres just right for the motel-casino he had in mind and after some bargaining offered him one thousand dollars an acre.

After he received the thirty-five-thousand-dollar check from Griffith, McAfee said to him: "If you'd bargained harder, I would've sold for less."

Griffith replied: "If you'd bargained harder, I would've paid more."

Morton Saiger, who spent his life working in casinos, recalled decades later: "Mr. McAfee, for a solid month, walked around showing everybody a cashier's check for thirty-five thousand dollars. He [was convinced] that he had caught a Texas sucker." By the 1980s, Saiger observed, it would be impossible to buy even a few inches of land on the Strip for a thousand dollars.

Griffith asked his nephew, architect William Moore, to supervise construction of an elaborate motel-casino. "The Last Frontier was conceived to be as near western as we could make it," Moore re-

"The Redlight District should, whenever it decides to move from its present location in the heart of the city, retire to a more secluded district. It should be retiring in demeanor and not flaunt itself in the face of the community."—*Las Vegas Age*, January 3, 1931

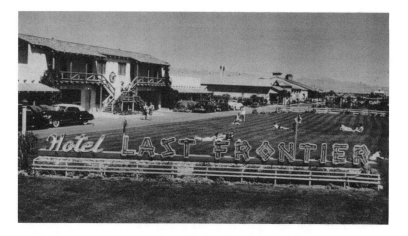

A Durable Survivor: The Last Frontier opened in 1942 and was expanded as the New Frontier in 1955. It became simply The Frontier in 1967 under a new owner, Howard Hughes. (Special Collections, UNLV Library)

"Most of Las Vegas's residents have come from somewhere else," wrote Mike Tronnes, editor of *Literary Las Vegas*. "In the early days, many came because what they were doing illegally at home was legal in Nevada. By simply crossing state lines, they were transformed into upstanding citizens."

called later. "The lobby had extremely high ceilings, with the fireplace running right up through the middle of it. The ceilings were of hewn timbers—rough-sawed boards antiqued in such a way as to look many years old."

A group of talented Navajos were brought from Gallup, New Mexico, to set stone that had been quarried in nearby Red Rock Canyon, and the Gay Nineties Bar was transferred from the old Arizona Club, "in the red light district in the heart of Las Vegas." The bar stools were carved to look like western saddles.

Because air conditioning had not yet been fully developed, the owners circulated cold water in tunnels under the hotel and installed pipes that carried the cold water through the walls of each room.

Under Uncle Sam's Watchful Eye

The builders of Griffith's Last Frontier ran into a major problem that Tom Hull had not faced in constructing the El Rancho. Because

World War II had begun, the U.S. government had set up a War Production Board with full control over building materials and wiring and plumbing supplies. Anyone who was planning major construction was required to prove that the proposed building would contribute to the war effort before he could get a permit to buy many materials.

William Moore managed to buy some wiring and plumbing materials despite those regulations, but inspectors who came out to take a look at the new structures going up weren't convinced that a Las Vegas casino would help win the war. The inspectors "essentially grabbed all the material having to do with anything electrical and took the material in trucks to the Army air base at Nellis," Moore recalled.

Desperate for wiring and conduits, the resourceful Moore arranged to buy two deserted mines in Pioche and sent crews there to "strip out wiring, casing, pipe, major control switches, even

Just Like the Movies: Away from the glitter, Las Vegas visitors in the 1950s could explore the countryside in a horse-drawn stagecoach. (Special Collections, UNR Library)

small switches" to use in the Last Frontier. The War Production Board would have seized all these building materials as well, if they had known about them, Moore realized. "That's the reason we made the deal on the basis that no reporting of the sale would ever be made."

Because millions of men and women were already serving in the Army, Navy, and Air Corps, and millions more were working in war industries, Moore found it difficult to hire building crews. Morton Saiger, who was then working for Moore, recalled: "I'd go downtown every morning at five, and pick up a bunch of winos . . . that were sitting there on the curb. Pick them up to come down for labor."

The Fatal Mistake

Saiger detected one major problem in the second Strip casino. "It was just ass-backwards," he said. "Bill Moore didn't visualize that the gambling was the main thing. They were catering to the hotel guests. When you came into the lobby, you always had to ask, 'Where's the casino?'

"You had to go across the dining room to go into the casino. There should have been no door or wall between the lobby and the casino. . . . When a guest checks in, his eyes should have been focused on the casino."

The explanation for this oversight was simple, Saiger said. "Mr. Griffith was not a casino man, and he figured if they wanted to gamble, they'll go outside or go through the dining room. It was very awkward. That was a very, very fatal mistake."

There was another problem, Saiger observed. "The Last Frontier catered to a lot of people, but not exactly. The gambling wasn't like the eastern people were used to. The people from Cleveland [the

Echoes of the Pony Express: At the Last Frontier hotel, Morton Saiger delivered mail on horseback. (Special Collections, UNR Library)

owners of a later very successful casino, the Desert Inn] attracted people from all over. It was a different type of gambling—No such thing as a $100 maximum. It was *gambling*. If you want $200, $300, $400 or $500, you were covered."

In some other ways, Griffith showed promise as a casino operator, Saiger observed. He organized the earliest junkets for California gamblers—first by bus, then by plane—and brought in Hollywood stars to perform in the Ramona Room and professionals to present melodramas in the Bird Cage Theater.

For six years Griffith managed to operate the Last Frontier successfully, but gambling remained a sideline for him, and he sold the casino in 1951 so he could concentrate on running hotels.

Meanwhile, Thomas Hull had run into major difficulties with El Rancho Vegas. "Unfortunately, managerial problems plagued the

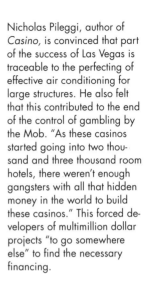

Nicholas Pileggi, author of *Casino,* is convinced that part of the success of Las Vegas is traceable to the perfecting of effective air conditioning for large structures. He also felt that this contributed to the end of the control of gambling by the Mob. "As these casinos started going into two thousand and three thousand room hotels, there weren't enough gangsters with all that hidden money in the world to build these casinos." This forced developers of multimillion dollar projects "to go somewhere else" to find the necessary financing.

High Rollers: Even in the early Las Vegas Strip casinos, gamblers won and lost fortunes at the tables. (Special Collections, UNLV Library)

Show of Shows: At Las Vegas High School, ca. 1958, teenage dancers rehearse their Rhythmette Review with student director Kenny Corey (left). Mary Lynn Ashworth, Phyllis Nelson (Barber), and Karen Sarret (left to right) were stars. It was "the most glamorous show in all of Nevada outside the hotels and casinos," in the mind of one young dancer. Years later, Phyllis Nelson Barber recalled the excitement in her memoir, *How I Got Cultured,* and a teacher's remark: "'Wholesome glamour,' Miss Stuckey claimed in an interview in the *Las Vegas Review-Journal.*" (Phyllis Barber Collection)

More horses pulled cozy carriages for newlyweds when they emerged from Las Vegas wedding chapels. (Special Collections, UNLV Library)

resort, resulting in a constant turnover of staff," Eugene P. Moehring reported. "Personality conflicts and administrative squabbles vanquished thirteen managers in the first three years alone." The pioneer who had first recognized the possibilities of the highway to Los Angeles sold "the trouble-plagued resort." Others also had troubles with El Rancho Vegas until Beldon Katleman bought it in 1947, redecorated and expanded it, and brought a few years of prosperity.

"Yet these halcyon days were short-lived," Moehring adds. "As the 1950s wore on, the El Rancho declined, outshined by its glittering new rivals on the Strip. A disastrous fire in 1960 mercifully closed the resort and it never reopened."

A New Era Begins

But the change Thomas Hull and R. E. Griffith had brought to Southern Nevada in the early 1940s was irreversible, even though neither of them recognized the full possibilities in their casinos.

Another much more flamboyant figure appeared on the Strip not long after the Last Frontier opened. His name was Benjamin Siegel, but he is remembered by the nickname he hated—Bugsy. His arrival marked the beginning of the most colorful period in the history of Las Vegas.

George Joseph, an experienced casino security executive, described his method of dealing with someone he suspected of cheating: "How ya doing?" he would ask. "My name's George Joseph. I'm with the casino. We counted up the chips here. You have $350,000 of our money. And you know what? We're not comfortable with your play. We've notified the Division of Gaming Enforcement. We've also notified your mother. What are you going to say to me now? You want to call me a name? Fine. But . . . I don't let you out. Not with our money."

Mafia Playground: After Bugsy Siegel's murder in Los Angeles, the Flamingo became a popular and profitable resort in the 1950s under the direction of Gus Greenbaum and his Mafia buddies. (Special Collections, UNLV Library)

7

BUGSY AND "THE BOYS"

Hoodlum with a Dream

By the time he was eighteen, Benjamin Siegel was already guilty of "assault, burglary, bookmaking, bootlegging, extortion, hijacking, murder, mayhem, narcotics, numbers, rape, white slavery . . . ," Deke Castleman writes in his guidebook *Las Vegas*.

"Bugsy was precocious in crime as some boys are precocious in music, art, or science," reporters Ed Reid and Ovid Demaris observed in *The Green Felt Jungle*. "His reckless disregard for danger, his wild antics, his ruthless contempt for the rights of others, his psychopathic temper—all these weaknesses became his greatest strength. He was feared and admired by every punk who knew him."

If Bugsy had stayed in New York, he might be remembered dimly today as a particularly vicious hitman—one of the more violent members of "Murder, Incorporated," trained to eliminate anyone who interfered with gang boss Meyer Lansky.

But in the early 1940s Lansky dispatched Bugsy to Los Angeles to get rid of some troublesome mobsters and to take over some of the most profitable gang operations, including control of the "wire" that brought the results of horse races, prize fights, football and basketball games, and other news that would interest gamblers in California and throughout the West.

Facing the Camera: New York gangster Benjamin Siegel moved up in the world from petty criminal to vicious hit man for the Mob. Then he came to Las Vegas and built the Flamingo. (Special Collections, UNLV Library)

Bugsy would make occasional visits to Las Vegas, gambling at the El Rancho and the Last Frontier, and by 1945 he began making plans to build a far more elaborate casino and motel.

Many of the people who met Bugsy in the West gained a much different impression of him than those who knew him during his life in New York as one of Meyer Lansky's most vicious enforcers.

"I've never met a more courtly, a more gentlemanly man in my life than Bugsy Siegel," singer Kay Starr said. "I was invited to sit down at the table and he was the first one to jump up to pull out my chair and I thought to myself, 'Well, if this is a gangster, I'd like to know more of them.'"

Rod Amateau, a film writer and director, recalled: "He was brought to the stage by [screen actor] George Raft . . . and he was very courteous and very nice, and later somebody told me, 'You know, he's a gangster.' Well, you know, as long as he doesn't, you know, shoot me, I'm not gonna judge him. You know, I mean, everybody's got to make a living.

"His handshake was very soft, as if he didn't want to hurt anything, didn't need to prove anything. It's later on that I realized that he was building this hotel in Las Vegas and I . . . cracked up, because . . . I'd been there, and I knew nobody can build a hotel in Las Vegas."

Comedian Alan King was still a boy when he met Bugsy and had similar doubts when Siegel talked about his plans for a casino he wanted to build out on a dusty stretch of the highway to Los Angeles. King just looked at him and thought to himself: "No wonder they call him Bugsy."

One of Bugsy's closest friends was Raft, then a world-famous star in gangster films. Raft sometimes spoke nostalgically of his own days on the edge of the law before he became an actor: "I was a bad pickpocket, but a good shoplifter."

Raft knew that Bugsy had earned his reputation as a murderous hood, but always spoke of him with affection—and copied some of Bugsy's mannerisms in his films. He observed the way Siegel combed his hair and said, "I did it the same way when I was playing a gangster." He also recalled Bugsy's extraordinary vanity: he usually wore a chin strap when he went to bed "to keep his profile looking good."

Raft was convinced that Siegel was trying to leave his gangster years behind him. "He came out here because he wanted to be somebody," Raft said. "Damn few people knew what made him tick, but I did. I thought he was a great guy."

Bugsy had a girlfriend named Virginia Hill, whom some remembered as a high-priced call girl. She had grown fond of the good life in California. When she and Bugsy spent a night at Raft's home, she brought her own silk sheets with her and usually brought along her personal maid as well.

Even though he was trying to blend into this new world of the rich and famous, Bugsy occasionally spoke candidly about his criminal past. Del Webb, a prominent builder who later became a casino owner, was startled when Siegel mentioned casually one day that he'd personally killed twelve men. When he noticed Webb's astonished expression, Bugsy laughed.

"There's no chance that you'd get killed," he reassured Webb. "We only kill each other."

As he made his plans for the Flamingo, Bugsy took a critical look at Tom Hull's El Rancho Vegas and R. E. Griffith's Last Frontier. Nicholas Pileggi, the author of *Casino*, observes: "The casinos that existed in Las Vegas pre-Siegel were cowboy casinos. When you went in . . . there was sawdust on the floor. Quite often they had donkeys . . . as part of the act. Siegel changed that."

Bugsy, who idolized movie stars and was deeply impressed by

"Ben Siegel took acting lessons," movie director Rod Amateau recalled. "He was very diligent, very serious about it. 'If Bogart can be a movie star, if Raft can be a movie star, if those two dwarves . . . Edward G. Robinson and Jimmy Cagney could be movie stars, why can't I?' he asked."

Miami Beach hotels, wanted to build a casino that would attract the most sophisticated gamblers from across the country and thought he understood what would persuade them to make the long trip to this isolated Nevada town. He persuaded Lucky Luciano and Meyer Lansky to back him by raising more than a million dollars in Mob money for his dream.

At first most Las Vegas businessmen did not know the source of Bugsy's cash. "At that time the community did not know, nor did the state know, that the money in the National Distillers was the money that Murder, Incorporated, had gone legitimate with," newspaperman John F. Cahlan said. "They had bought the National Distillers so they could pour their gang money into a legitimate proposition."

Cahlan, who became well acquainted with Bugsy during his early months in Las Vegas because both patronized a health club on Fremont Street, remembered him as a very handsome man who dressed with great care. Cahlan helped Siegel make one very useful acquaintance.

"Benny and I used to meet in the steam room . . . a couple of times a week," Cahlan recalled. "At the time, the county commissioners had not been approached for a license for the Flamingo Hotel. I had learned from one of the commissioners that he was going to vote against the license." Cahlan passed along word about this potential problem to Siegel and set up a special meeting between Bugsy and the politician. The newspaperman was not sure exactly what happened at the secret meeting—but the commissioner suddenly changed sides and voted in Bugsy's favor.

Siegel first tried to buy the El Cortez Hotel in Downtown Las Vegas, but some city officials (who by this time had learned of his criminal career) made it clear he would not get their help in obtaining the utilities he would need to expand and improve the hotel. Then he found a place outside the city limits where his new resort could use well water and generate its own power and thus not depend on any help from the city administration.

Billy Wilkerson, the owner of several fine Sunset Strip clubs and founder of the *Hollywood Reporter,* had started constructing a hotel-casino far out on highway 91 but had run out of money after spending $600,000 on the ambitious undertaking. Siegel took over the unfinished building and began turning Wilkerson's project into a luxurious hotel-casino modeled on his own memories of the most elaborate Florida resorts.

His friends were still skeptical. "You're gonna have to buy some camels to carry the gamblers out to that sandy strip," one of his fellow mobsters told him.

The Fatal Overrun

The one million dollars Bugsy's gangster friends had agreed to supply, after some hesitation, was quickly spent, then two million, then three million, and finally six and a half million dollars.

One often-repeated story is that Siegel, the tough New York gangster, was being taken by crooked suppliers in Las Vegas. They would sell him a carload of building materials during the morning, get someone to sneak onto the site and steal the same materials during the night, and then resell him the same carload of bricks or lumber or other supplies the next day.

That might have been part of the problem, but his own extravagance also contributed substantially to the steadily rising cost. "The Flamingo had landscaped lawns and gardens studded with palm trees, an elegant waterfall by its front entrance, plus a variety of distractions for its guests including a pool, health club, tennis and golf, stabling for forty horses, show rooms and shops," David Spanier

"I was just a young boy, and [Siegel] looked up and down this main drag which had tumbleweeds on it and said, 'Kid, some day there'll be fifty hotels,' and I turned aside, and I said to myself, 'No wonder they call him Bugsy.'"
—Comedian Alan King

writes in *Welcome to the Pleasuredome.* "The hotel, low and spacious, had only 105 rooms but reeked of luxury."

Although Bugsy's extravagance in building his desert showcase was obvious, the men around Meyer Lansky suspected that not all the money was going into the Flamingo. During the construction period, Bugsy's girlfriend made a trip or two to Europe, and the mobsters were convinced that she had taken along a suitcase full of their money to deposit in a secret Swiss bank account. While there is no clear proof that Bugsy was cheating his investors, their suspicion was enough.

"At a meeting of the bosses in Havana on Christmas Day, 1946, a vote was taken," Deke Castleman writes. "If the Flamingo was a success, Siegel would be reprieved, and given a chance to pay back the huge loan. If it failed . . . *muerta.*"

Everything went wrong on the casino's opening day, December 26, 1946. Many of Bugsy's Hollywood friends failed to make the trip out to Las Vegas on a wet, wintry day. Some who were ready to fly out were stranded in Los Angeles because of flight cancellations. The Flamingo motel itself was far from finished, so those who did arrive had to be put up in the competing motel-casinos, the El Rancho and the Last Frontier.

After the opening night, expensive entertainers were sometimes performing to eight or nine guests. Losses were so heavy during the first two weeks that Bugsy had to close down.

Virginia Hill was off on one of her mysterious trips. Bugsy went to spend a few days in her luxurious home in Beverly Hills. One evening he was talking quietly with an old friend, Al Smiley (known as Smiley the Russian). Virginia's nineteen-year-old brother was in an upstairs bedroom with a girlfriend.

Reid and Demaris report in *The Green Felt Jungle:*

Entertainer Rose Marie had a different recollection of the opening night of Bugsy Siegel's Flamingo than many others who were there. "Opening night was fantastic," she says. "Jewels and diamonds, everybody was there, everybody in tuxedos, it was just grand." But then: "The third day all the stars went back and we were working to nine or ten people in the dining room. . . . To see Jimmy Durante working to nine or ten people was really very strange."

According to the police, the killer had waited for Bugsy in the shadow of a rose-covered pergola with a 30-caliber Army carbine. He had rested the barrel of the carbine on a crossbar of the latticework, sighted, and carefully squeezed off the entire clip. Nine slugs slammed through a 14-inch pane of glass. Siegel, who had been sitting directly in front of an undraped window, his head illuminated by a table lamp behind the sofa, had taken four of the slugs—two in the head and two in the chest. Five went wild, shattering a marble statue of Bacchus on the grand piano and puncturing a painting of a nude holding a wine glass. . . .

On the floor between his legs, detectives found a copy of the *Los Angeles Times*, given to Bugsy after he had had dinner at a restaurant called Jack's-at-the-Beach. Clipped to the top of the first page of the paper was a card. Printed on it were the words: "Good night. Sleep peacefully with compliments of Jack."

The funeral was held two days later. Although he had devoted the last years of his life to making friends with famous people, especially actors and actresses, only five mourners showed up for the brief service.

"I'll never forget how I was told that Benny Siegel was killed," Alan King recalled. "Someone said to me: 'Benny took a cab.' That was the line. 'Benny took a cab.' See, nobody ever died. . . . When the news came out, a guy looked at me and said, 'What took 'em so long?'"

"The Boys" Take Over a Town

About twenty minutes after Bugsy was murdered in California, three men showed up at the Flamingo in Las Vegas.

"We're taking over here," one of them told the casino staff.

Gus Greenbaum, who had wide experience in gambling management, soon took control and turned the Flamingo into an exceptionally profitable business for its next seven years. Many other gangland figures moved in to build new Las Vegas casinos during the 1940s and 1950s, some with extraordinary success.

"Casino executives linked to the mob had an instinctive feel and flair for gambling, acquired via illegal bookmaking," David Spanier observes.

Speaking of these new arrivals, gaming control official Robbins Cahill commented: "The people that were coming to Las Vegas were not bishops of the church or pillars of the community." Some of them were more acceptable to Las Vegans than others, however. Cahill himself approved of Moe Dalitz, a former bootlegger who also had a record of running illegal gambling operations in Cleveland. "The guys from Cleveland were silk glove men," Cahill said approvingly.

He was less impressed by Benny Binion, who had a long criminal record and had faced two charges of murder in Texas (but had not been convicted). Cahill liked Binion personally but felt that he should never have been licensed to run a Nevada casino.

Investigators later discovered that Las Vegas had been declared an "open city" by the Mafia soon after gambling was legalized in Nevada in 1931. As the activity increased, at least twenty-four Mafia families divided up control of various enterprises. Each family had permission to take part in skimming profits from the casinos, but after a while the Chicago mob became the dominant family along the Strip.

The Mafia families were given credit by some citizens for keeping the town relatively quiet and crime free. George L. Ullom, an early resident, said: "Apparently the word was out, 'Look, if you're going to do something, you don't do it in Las Vegas. Keep Las Vegas clean.'"

This policy led to the custom of choosing quiet desert spots some distance from the town to dispose of the bodies of those who became troublesome to the Mob. Susan Berman, daughter of gangster David Berman, recalls one such episode. Two young men who had just been released from prison in Nevada found themselves short of cash and stopped to rob a casino. As they made their escape, orders went out to kill them "as soon as they crossed to California"—but not to touch them as long as they were anywhere near Las Vegas.

"It was like we had two police forces," Bob Stupak, former chairman of the board of the Stratosphere Tower Corporation, observed. "We had the regular police, you know, and we had the boys."

"No one got killed that wasn't supposed to," actress and hotel owner Debbie Reynolds recalls of this period. "And we were never frightened of anything of that sort."

Stupak is convinced that the presence of gangsters in Las Vegas actually became something of a tourist attraction. "I mean when

"Many of the men who started casinos were not gangsters in the cigar and machine gun tradition that people seem to think they were. They [were] professional gamblers who were illegal gamblers in Miami, illegal gamblers in Cleveland and Massachusetts [who] could all of a sudden go to Las Vegas and be legitimate."
—Nicholas Pileggi, author of *Casino*

Front Man: Wilbur Clark created the Desert Inn and made it "one of the classiest joints in town," with the help of Mafia money and Moe Dalitz from the Cleveland Mob. (Special Collections, UNLV Library)

Presidential Arrival: When President John F. Kennedy came to Las Vegas in the early 1960s—a time when his brother, Attorney General Robert Kennedy, was relentlessly pursuing members of the Mob—politicians and military officers greeted the Chief. (Special Collections, UNLV Library)

you came here, you know, you thought every time you saw a guy with a violin case, there was a tommy gun in there. And there was a hood behind every tree just looking out."

Fooling the Tax Collectors

During the late 1940s and the 1950s, owners concealed much of their casino income to avoid paying taxes on it. This practice of skimming added substantially to the Mob's profits.

"The early skim started because the casino owners had to pay back a lot of their early investors and a lot of those investors gave you cash," says Nicholas Pileggi. "They didn't want any checks. No checks, Charlie, no checks."

Susan Berman remembers going into the counting room with her father and watching as the owners divided up the ones, fives, tens and hundreds: "I saw them go—three for us, one for the government, two for Meyer [Lansky]. I helped them count the bills . . . the skimming, of course it was a crime. But it wasn't a crime like having to kill people."

Later, when the Gaming Control Board raided the Stardust, "they uncovered a secret vault, packed with bags of coins, which had been systematically diverted from the slots, night after night," Spanier reports. The owners had set up a fake weighing machine to conceal their skimming.

Dennis Gomes, head of the audit division for the control board, recalled how dangerous it was to interfere with such scams. "I got a gun in the stomach when we broke up the Stardust scam," Gomes said.

A similar scheme had been introduced at the Fremont, and mobsters had managed to hide twelve million dollars a year in untaxed income from the two casinos, one expert estimates.

"All those old guys were cheaters," casino owner Jackie Gaughan said. "They thought you had to cheat. They didn't know about percentages, they probably couldn't figure percentages. So they didn't know the strength of the game."

The Hidden Owners

"Today, the big mystery is the identity of the owners of the Sahara Hotel, newest of the multimillion dollar casino palaces along the Strip," one magazine writer observed in 1954. The three listed own-

""My mother had the reaction probably every wife coming to Las Vegas [had]. She said, 'Is this all?' And my father . . . took her off the train and said, 'Betty, this is where we're going to build Paradise.' . . . My father and all his friends were criminals from the time they were eleven or twelve. So I think for many of these men Las Vegas was their last chance. And they were determined in their forties . . . to do it right."—Susan Berman, daughter of gangster David Berman

Nobody talked about the backgrounds of the owners or the casino managers or whatever," comedian Alan King recalled about the 1930s and 1940s. "Vegas was like another planet, and all of a sudden all the things that were illegal all over the country became not only acceptable—it was what drove this town."

ers were small-time gamblers out of Oregon, he wrote, but obviously none of them had the money or experience to run a major enterprise. "The only thing that figures is they're backed by somebody big."

Discovering "Mr. Big" was always difficult, and sometimes impossible. In *The Green Felt Jungle* Ed Reid and Ovid Demaris examine a bloody episode in New York City that revealed "one of the most celebrated examples of hidden ownership": "On the evening of May 2, 1957, a fat gunman waited for his victim in the foyer of a fashionable apartment house on Central Park West. When the victim appeared, the gunman, coming up behind him, shouted: 'This is for you, Frank!' . . . There was a roar, and Frank Costello, known as the prime minister of organized crime in America, staggered sideways, blood streaming down his cheek. . . . Costello . . . sank onto a leather-covered bench . . . 'Somebody tried to get me,' he mumbled."

Costello was rushed to a nearby hospital, and while doctors were removing a .38 slug from behind his right ear, detectives searched the pockets of his jacket and slacks. They found a slip of paper with some revealing handwritten notes: "Gross casino wins as of 4/27/57, $651,284; Casino wins less markers, $434,695; Slot wins, $62,844; Markers, $153,745."

Clearly Costello—who would have been barred automatically from ownership or control of any Nevada casino because of his known criminal history—was getting detailed inside information from one that was enormously profitable. But which one?

With help from the Nevada Gaming Control Board, detectives soon discovered that the $651,284 figure "matched perfectly the gross casino receipts for the Tropicana Hotel for the first 24 days of its operation," Reid and Demaris report.

Except for the shot fired by the "fat gunman," the gangster's concealed ownership might have been kept hidden for years. Once it was revealed, Costello's associates were ordered to sell their interests.

A Tough Guy from Chicago

As long as the Mob in distant cities controlled many casinos, one problem was choosing someone who could be trusted to oversee skimming and to pick reliable couriers to transport suitcases filled with money back to New York or Chicago or Detroit.

For several years the boys from Chicago assigned that job to Anthony Spilotro, who was called "Tony the Ant" because of his baby face and his height—he was just five feet, five inches tall.

"Spilotro was a suspect in 25 murders, but was never convicted," Seth Rosenfeld reported in the *San Francisco Examiner*. He allegedly carried out one of the murders by putting a fellow gang member's head in a vise and slowly tightening it. His "most important function was to break legs or kill anybody who got out of line," said Bill Roemer of the Chicago Crime Commission.

But then he decided to launch his own crime spree in Las Vegas. Ignoring the general Mob policy of keeping the town clean, he formed an odd group that was called the "Hole in the Wall Gang" because they sometimes staged burglaries by actually breaking through walls to get to the cash hidden inside business premises.

"Before that time we'd never had anybody that was associated with organized crime come out and conduct criminal activity at the street level," recalled Bob Miller, who was then district attorney and later became governor of Nevada.

Some mobsters apparently decided that Spilotro's reckless behavior might endanger their gambling enterprises, which were bringing in millions.

Wheel of Fortune: When he opened the Flamingo in 1946, Bugsy Siegel expected to change the Las Vegas image from folksy Western to sophisticated glamor, but his roulette wheels failed to attract glittering crowds of big spenders. Fifty years later, new Las Vegas casinos are closer to Bugsy's dream. An international mix of gamblers bet fortunes at the roulette wheels. (Glen Marullo)

A Mysterious Disappearance

One June day, Anthony Spilotro and his brother Michael, who were in Chicago, stepped into Anthony's car and went for a drive. Nine days later, a farmer who was spreading weed killer over his cornfield in Indiana discovered two bodies. They were soon identified as the Spilotro brothers.

In the years between his rise to dominance in Las Vegas and his sudden disappearance from Chicago, something had affected the Mob's view of Tony the Ant. Las Vegas reporters noticed that no Mafia leaders attended his funeral, and the fact that he was buried quietly was seen as proof that he had been killed "without respect."

Another Menace

In disposing of Tony the Ant, the bosses had quietly eliminated one threat to their profitable enterprises in Las Vegas. But another danger had appeared just after the end of World War II, and it was beyond their control.

This new menace could have frightened away some of the hundreds of thousands of visitors who were just beginning to choose Las Vegas as their playground. But instead of worrying about the danger, casino owners and other businessmen presented it to the world as a novelty and used it to publicize the growing town.

In 1997, a short street in northwest Las Vegas was named "Siegal Circle." (The name on the street sign is misspelled.)

Picture of the Week in *Life* magazine for November 12, 1951, showed an atomic cloud clearly visible behind neon signs in Downtown Las Vegas. (Las Vegas News Bureau)

The Secret Visitors

Early in 1951, a group of strangers began making periodic visits to Las Vegas. They would arrive by plane, register quietly at the Last Frontier, get a few hours' sleep, and then head north from the city around two A.M.

At first, few Las Vegans knew who the visitors were. But they did notice that a day or two after their arrival a brilliant, almost blinding light would appear in the distance, and that a strange cloud would be visible in the skies.

When the *Las Vegas Review-Journal* began publishing stories explaining that the mushroom-shaped clouds were caused by aboveground atomic tests, as some Las Vegans had guessed, the FBI suspected that someone working at the atomic test site was giving away security secrets.

"I don't know how they could hide the thing, because the intense light that it spreads was seen as far off as San Francisco or Los Angeles," *Review-Journal* editor John F. Cahlan said years later. But after the paper's second or third story was published, he recalled, "We had FBI people in here, investigating me and my news staff, because they wanted to find out where the leak was."

Actually, Cahlan said, the newspaper did not have to depend on confidential sources for any of its stories, including the one about the first device, which was set off in the greatest of secrecy.

"The Atomic Energy Commission took every precaution that they could," Cahlan recalled. "Unfortunately, however, they could not control traffic, which was very heavy from California to here, and a truck driver saw the explosion as he was coming down the hill toward Stateline, and he got into Jean, and he very nicely called the *Review-Journal*, and we got an eyewitness account of the blast."

As a result of that unexpected revelation, the AEC tightened its security further, hoping to continue experiments in secrecy. But the *Review-Journal* continued to report each blast.

"It was very simple," Cahlan said. "These scientists would all of a sudden start flying into Las Vegas from Alamogordo or Albuquerque, and there would be a great deal of activity at both Nellis Air Force Base and Indian Springs. And the scientists would be billeted at the Hotel Last Frontier and would leave calls for two o'clock in the morning. Well, when ten or fifteen scientists leave calls for two o'clock in the morning, then something is going to happen.

"So, I just told the FBI 'We've got a bellhop out at the Last Frontier that calls us and tells us there have been calls left for two or three in the morning. So we were able to pinpoint the shots, at least the day that they were set off."

After the first few explosions, Cahlan recalled, "Half the city of Las Vegas would get up in the morning and go out on the flat above the valley out there, to watch the blasts go off and had a very good view of them."

After a while, both residents and visiting gamblers began to accept the sequence of blasts as a part of the city's daily life. "The people in the casinos would be gambling and so forth, and they'd see the big flash of light, and they'd say, 'Well, there goes another one,' and go back to their crap games."

Cahlan was later invited to go out to Frenchman's Flat, sixty-five miles northwest of Las Vegas, and provided with some special

"The players . . . really don't mind. It's doubtful if any of them, especially those who are winning good or badly stuck, would notice the A-bomb if the AEC boys touched one off in Bugsy Siegel's old chartreuse suite in the plushy Flamingo. There are too many important things on their mind to worry about that kind of inconsequential horseplay."
—Bob Considine, quoted by Jefferson Graham in *Vegas: Live and In Person*

glasses so he could get a closer look at one of the tests. Four decades later he left a vivid description of what he saw and felt:

> It was the most awesome thing I have ever seen. The device is exploded, and you see this terrific flash of white light, and then there is a rolling purple ball. The smoke just seems to roll around the ball, and as the ball grows bigger, it turns into all colors of the rainbow, and then, all of a sudden, the sound of the shock wave'd hit you, and it's just as if somebody took a bat and hit you in the stomach. It could very easily knock a man over if he weren't expecting it. And all the time, this roiling, boiling cloud—or fireball—is rising in the air and picking up the dirt off the ground. It seems to suck the dirt from the ground into the stem of the mushroom.
>
> The most awesome thing is the red fire, because it looks like the fires that Dante describes in the *Inferno*. It's too bad that these people that are thinking about starting a war can't

Mushroom clouds on the horizon north of Las Vegas gave away the secret. Atomic bombs were being tested above ground at Frenchman's Flat, attracting sightseers who ignored the danger. (Nevada Historical Society)

"I don't know exactly how much the bomb had to do with it, but around shot time the play in our casino seemed to go up and the drinking got heavier," Wilbur Clark of the Desert Inn told a *New Yorker* writer. "The curious thing was that guests would drive here from L.A. to see a shot and then not bother to look at it. I'd instruct my pit-men to let the players at their tables know when it was about time for the flash, but the players would go right on with their games."

see the atomic explosion—because if they'd ever see that, they'd back off in a hurry.

But for decades the Las Vegas newspapers rarely raised a question about the safety of the atomic and nuclear tests. Cahlan recalled that the *Review-Journal* "conditioned the local people for the explosions that were to follow" and focused on the prospect that nuclear power "was going to unlock new eras."

Complaints made by victims of the testing were quickly dismissed. When a farmer whose property was downwind from the testing area said his goats had turned blue after one of the explosions, the AEC told him that "the blue color was caused by the goats rubbing against the zinc coating of his fences," although he had never noticed that effect before.

When a lone conservative Republican member of the state legislature introduced a resolution to stop atomic tests at the Nevada Test Site, the *Las Vegas Sun* responded angrily: "Who shall get out of Nevada, the AEC or the crackpot who makes such a suggestion in public?"

Senator Pat McCarran of Nevada often expressed his enthusiasm for the millions of dollars in federal money pouring into the state and the hundreds of jobs the test site provided for Nevadans. One historian reports that McCarran had "worked hard to convince the Atomic Energy Commission and President Harry Truman to move the atomic test site from the Bikini Atoll [where the first tests were carried out] to Southern Nevada."

Governor Charles Russell joined in celebrating the bombs and seemed to consider this the ideal use of a sizeable part of the state he governed. "It's exciting to think," he said in 1952, "that the sub-marginal land of the proving ground is furthering science and helping national defense. We had long ago written off that terrain as wasteland, and today it's blooming with atoms."

Come See Our Atomic Explosion

Many Las Vegas businesses realized that the blasts could be used as a way to attract more visitors to the city. They experimented with a variety of methods to focus attention on the dramatic bomb tests.

The Flamingo beauty parlor offered visiting gamblers an "Atomic hairdo." The Sands staged a contest to choose "Miss Atomic

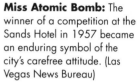

Miss Atomic Bomb: The winner of a competition at the Sands Hotel in 1957 became an enduring symbol of the city's carefree attitude. (Las Vegas News Bureau)

Bomb." A furniture store filled a barrel with shards of broken window glass and invited customers to take away the pieces as "Atomic Bomb Souvenirs." The Atomic View Motel promised guests that they could watch the next explosion in comfort between swims in the motel swimming pool. Other motels offered special "atomic box lunches" for visitors who wished to drive closer to the bomb site for a picnic.

The Las Vegas Chamber of Commerce printed special atomic calendars, with dates of future tests marked so visitors could plan their holidays to include the spectacle. For years Clark County used a mushroom-shaped explosion as the central feature on the county seal.

(The fascination with atomic bombs was evident in Las Vegas long before the Nevada tests began. A bar had mixed vodka, brandy, champagne, and sherry to create an "atomic cocktail" just hours after the bombing of Hiroshima.)

Sacrificed Swine and Doom Towns

Few Las Vegans knew in detail about the exercises being carried out by the U.S. military and the Atomic Energy Commission on the tightly guarded test site.

The most detailed account of what was happening sixty-five miles to the northwest is provided by A. Costandina Titus in *Bombs in the Backyard.* "One particularly bizarre experiment became known as the 'Charge of the Swine Brigade,'" she wrote. "To determine which fabrics afforded the best protection from burns, the army fitted 111 White Chester pigs in specially tested uniforms with seams, zippers and drawstrings matched exactly to the specifications of the army's own standard GI-issue field jackets. The pigs were then exposed to the blasts of two successive shots. Seventy-two of the pigs were killed outright, but the army was still able to gain what it considered valuable information about the thermal protection properties of its uniforms."

Later, elaborate "doom towns" were constructed near ground zero. "Full-scale homes were built and furnished with everything from brand-name foods in the refrigerator to current magazines on the coffee table," Titus reports. "Late model automobiles stood in carports and mannequins wearing the latest ready-made fashions were strategically placed throughout in lifelike situations."

Review-Journal reporter Archie Teague provided a vivid report on the result of one of these experiments: "People played by dummies lay dead and dying in basements, living rooms, kitchens, bedrooms. . . . A mannequin mother died horribly in her one-story house of precast concrete slabs. Portions of her plaster and paint body were found in three different areas. A mannequin tot . . . was blown out of bed and showered with needle-sharp fragments. . . . A simulated mother was blown to bits in the act of feeding her infant baby food."

In the spring of 1953, the Atomic Energy Commission conducted three "dirty" experiments that caused heavy radioactive fallout over much of Southern Utah.

On the morning of one of the shots residents of St. George, Utah, were advised to stay indoors until noon, and automobiles belonging to residents there were washed down after the explosion.

Several large flocks of sheep were en route to their lambing sheds that morning, one historian reported. "Of the 11,710 sheep grazing in the contaminated zone 40 miles north and 160 miles west of the test site, 1,410 lambing ewes and 2,970 new lambs died within weeks of the three shots."

No Secret: Airborne cameras revealed the location of the Nevada Test Site long before it became the target of complaints from victims of radiation poisoning. (Nevada Historical Society)

Decades after such detailed evidence of the frightening results of an atomic explosion had been recorded, Thomas K. Jones, deputy under-secretary of defense, was still telling Nevadans and other Americans how to survive a nuclear war: "Dig a hole, cover it with a couple of doors and then throw three feet of dirt on top. . . . If there are enough shovels to go around, everybody's going to make it."

Vern Willis, a former president of the Las Vegas Chamber of Commerce, told one historian that the Atomic Energy Commission had reassured him that the mountains north of Las Vegas "would shield the city from any potentially dangerous fallout." Actually, that historian notes, "it was really the prevailing southwesterlies that saved the city."

The Brave Generals

As a result of the tests in southern Nevada, "small towns became gardens of leukemia," Michael Ventura states. "Somebody . . . told me that especially after the first few blasts . . . the horses wouldn't eat. Cats wouldn't let themselves be scratched. Dogs wouldn't let themselves be touched."

The most startling experiment described by A. Costandina Titus risked the lives of thousands of American soldiers.

Five thousand soldiers were asked to assume that two different enemy armies had invaded the United States and had managed to drive U.S. forces down to Southern Nevada. To avoid defeat, the Americans were ordered to respond by first using an atomic bomb to blast a hole in the enemy lines, then to pursue the fleeing enemy forces.

This "scenario" was used to explain to the U.S. soldiers why they were being ordered to cross the area where the bomb had been exploded almost immediately after the blast. While the soldiers were warned about reptiles and snakes in the desert area, they received no warning about the danger of their exposure to radiation.

The Atomic Energy Commission had previously prohibited stationing anyone closer than six miles from a blast. The U.S. Army soon overruled that safeguard, moving troops to within two miles of the blast. It then began urging that soldiers be moved closer and closer to ground zero to give commanding officers realistic experience in fighting a war in which atomic weapons were being used. This led to the experiment that sent five thousand men over miles of dangerously radioactive desert land.

After exposing the men to radiation, a brigadier general boasted about the experiment: "In this exercise, for the first time in known history, troops successfully attacked directly toward ground zero immediately following the atomic explosion."

The First Doubters

During the 1950s and 1960s, a few voices were heard in opposition to atomic testing. Ex-soldiers who had been subjected to various military experiments began suing the U.S. government, but most of them died before their cases were settled.

One of the strongest opponents was scientist Linus Pauling, who estimated that ten thousand people "had died or were dying from leukemia because of the nuclear tests."

Then, in 1968, one of the richest men in the world, and by far the most influential man in Nevada, joined the battle to end the tests.

Mysterious Billionaire:
In his younger days, before moving to Las Vegas, Howard Hughes was a successful aviation tycoon, controlling stockholder in Trans World Airlines. (Special Collections, UNLV Library)

9

MR. HUGHES ARRIVES IN LAS VEGAS

Arrival Before Dawn

During Thanksgiving weekend in 1966, an unusually short train stopped on the outskirts of Las Vegas at four A.M., Sunday, November 27. The train carried a strange cargo: Howard Hughes, a reclusive billionaire who had come "to make Nevada his kingdom . . . and to create a world he could control completely," one of his biographers reported.

Hughes had started cross-country from Boston three days earlier on a carefully selected express train, but when it reached Ogden, Utah, he was reminded that even a billionaire's best-laid plans could go astray. The train came to a dead halt. When his aides asked for an explanation, they were told laconically: "Equipment breakdown."

Vastly irritated but undaunted, Hughes gave one of his carefully selected Mormon aides firm instructions to see that his trip continued without delay. The aide rented a locomotive. Hughes's two private cars were then separated from the rest of the train and attached to the substitute hauler, and the secret journey to Las Vegas ended just slightly behind schedule.

Hughes and his aides had assumed that not many people were likely to be roaming around the train junction at that hour, and they were right. No stranger seemed to observe the thin, pale, trembling

"In 1966 Howard pointed out to me that he was sick and tired of being a small fish in the growing big pond of Southern California and wanted to be the big fish in the small pond of Nevada," recalled Robert Maheu, who became chief executive officer for Hughes's Nevada operations.

bearded man being taken off the train on a stretcher and lifted into a waiting van.

As he was driven across town to the Strip, the richest man in the world had a brief look at the city he had decided to reshape. Because of something that had happened just five months earlier, he had all the cash he needed to carry out his ambitious plans.

Becoming Even Richer

"He was a figure of gothic horror," Michael Drosnin wrote in *Citizen Hughes,* basing the description on interviews with two of Howard Hughes's Mormon aides and the only doctor to see him periodically between 1968 and 1970. "Emaciated, practically skeletal, with only 120 pounds stretched out over his six-feet-four-inch frame, and hardly a speck of color about him anywhere, not even in his lips. . . . Only the long gray hair that trailed halfway down his back, the thin, scraggly beard that reached midway onto his sunken chest, and the hideously long nails that extended several inches."

In May 1966, the largest check ever made out to an individual— $546,549,171—was delivered to Hughes in exchange for his controlling shares in Trans World Airlines, which he had been forced to sell after a long, bitter quarrel with fellow stockholders.

As often happened with Hughes, his reluctant action in accepting that settlement occurred at just the right moment for him— when the stock was at its peak. But because of the huge cash payment, he faced the danger of having to pay millions in federal and state income taxes unless he could put most of that money in some active investment without much delay.

A man who had managed to live without paying one cent in federal income taxes in seventeen years, according to biographer Michael Drosnin, Hughes was determined to avoid what he saw as an unjustified penalty. To escape heavy California state taxes, he immediately abandoned his two California mansions and his luxurious hotel suites in Los Angeles and began planning to move to a place that was friendlier to billionaires. He considered four possibilities: the Bahamas, the Mediterranean, England—or Las Vegas.

Hughes always hesitated before taking any step—major or minor. While considering which of the four refuges to choose, he traveled three thousand miles—to Massachusetts—to work out detailed plans before selecting his new home. In Boston, he and his aides took over the fifth floor of the Ritz-Carlton Hotel. Elevator operators were given orders not to allow other hotel guests to get off on that floor, and the knob was removed from the fifth floor fire doors, so no one could gain access by coming up or down the fire stairs.

This side trip to Boston cost him at least a quarter of a million dollars, and it took him eighteen weeks to make up his mind. But just before Thanksgiving 1966, he boarded a luxurious private car for the trip to his new western home.

The Unhappy Billionaire

The Howard Hughes who was about to revolutionize Las Vegas was deeply depressed by the time he reached Nevada.

He often recorded his towering rages at the hundreds of men who were on his personal payroll, holding them personally responsible for everything that went wrong in his life. In one famous memo, he concentrated on the sins of Bill Gay, his chief of staff, and the dozens of people who worked at an administrative office the Hughes empire maintained on Romaine Street in Los Angeles. Focusing on what most people might have considered a minor inconvenience, he wrote at length, and with growing irritation, about the latest outrage—the failure of Gay's assistants to provide him with his favorite magazines:

"When I agreed to being [Howard Hughes's] alter-ego, maybe I made a serious mistake as far as his world was concerned," his chief aide, Robert Maheu, commented later. "It enabled him the luxury of going into a cocoon with the progression of time. It was very difficult for him to understand [the] reality [of] the outside world."

> I want these aviation magazines and I requested them four days ago and it is just ludicrous that I have not received them. There is *Aviation Week, Aviation, Aero Digest, Flying*. . . . [T]here are countless magazines in this country and an equal number in England and France and for me to sit here for four days and have two issues of one British magazine and one is-

sue of one American magazine, this is just absolutely ludicrous. They didn't even get me a copy of *Flight*—they didn't get me any copy of any U.S. magazine until after 48 hours, whereas during that time a simple trip to one of the airports would have obtained at least *Flying*. This is just absolutely appalling to me. . . . This is typical of our whole slovenly indifferent way this entire operation of mine is handled. . . . It just saps at my guts and my ailing constitution. The damage it does to my system physiologically is beyond imagination. I am telling you I would be better off if I did not have the assistance of that Romaine Street office. . . . I want to know why my office has to be so completely inefficient, inadequate, careless, indifferent, ineffective, slovenly, and Christ Almighty it is now four days since my request.

The same man who failed to make sure that he got his aviation magazines was also responsible for ruining his doomed marriage to the film star Jean Peters, Hughes declared in another memo addressed to a different aide: "Bill's total indifference and laxity to my pleas for help in my domestic area, voiced urgently to him, week by week throughout the past seven to eight years, have resulted in a complete, I am afraid irrevocable loss of my wife. I blame Bill completely for this unnecessary debacle. I feel he let me down—utterly, totally, completely."

The Unwelcome Guest

In Las Vegas, Hughes's aides had arranged for him to have the use of two floors of the Desert Inn until the Christmas rush began. The owners of the famous old resort were not as thrilled by the presence of Mr. Hughes and his staff of faithful Mormon assistants as

outsiders might expect. While they knew Hughes was good for the substantial rent, neither the reclusive billionaire nor any of his staff were ever seen at the tables or the slots. And they were occupying suites that would ordinarily be used to attract and reward high rollers.

As the weeks went by and the Hughes entourage showed no sign of moving on, Morris (Moe) Dalitz, one of the four owners of the Desert Inn, grew impatient. "We had already confirmed many reservations for those two floors, in anticipation of Mr. Hughes moving on," Dalitz recalled later.

After some hesitation, the hotel's managers ordered the world's richest man to leave. But instead of checking out, Hughes casually bought control of the hotel—for $13.2 million.

That marked the beginning of the biggest buying spree in the history of Nevada. But before Hughes could take over operations at the Desert Inn he faced a major hurdle: approval by the Nevada Gaming Control Board.

Ordinarily this would take months and would require that Hughes appear personally before the gaming authorities to answer questions about "all aspects of his personal and business life." One historian recalls that Hughes had an absolute horror of testifying before any official body, partly because of "a very tumultuous appearance before the House Un-American Activities Committee during the Joe McCarthy era, when he still owned RKO Studios."

He knew from some of his earlier experiences that the rules that governed ordinary men could be waived if he sent his representatives to speak strongly enough and persuasively enough to the right people.

They did.

Ignoring all the rules they had set up to prevent Mob control of casinos, Nevada's Gaming Control Board certified Hughes as the new owner without requiring him to pass any of the standard tests. Robert Maheu, a former FBI man whom Hughes paid half a million dollars a year to oversee his Nevada ventures, remembers receiving a call from the boss he never met shortly after the Desert Inn project was okayed.

"How many more of these toys are available?" Hughes asked him.

Many were, it turned out—and Hughes bought four more of them in a few months, paying what many insiders considered very high prices. The Mob bosses were eager to sell for a variety of reasons. Some of them were old enough to retire. Others were afraid that future congressional investigations might force them out of business because of their criminal backgrounds, even though Nevada authorities had forgiven them their earlier trespasses. And some of them realized they were unlikely to find another buyer who would pay cash—and who was not adept at analyzing the possible future hard times for the aging casinos. In less than a year Hughes bought the Sands, the Castaways, and the Frontier.

The most surprising purchase was a tiny casino called the Silver Slipper, which attracted a few passing gamblers by displaying a huge, brightly lighted slipper that revolved endlessly through the night.

Claudine Williams, who was then co-owner of the insignificant little casino, later recalled why Hughes bought it. "He was at the penthouse of the Desert Inn, which was directly across the street from the Silver Slipper," she said. "So, with the revolving of the slipper, the shadows would hit [his] window, and disturbed his rest. Mr. Maheu showed us a telegram Mr. Hughes had sent to him: 'I want you to buy that place, that damn sign is driving me crazy, it goes round and round and round.'"

It cost him $5,360,000 to get a good night's sleep in his Desert Inn hideaway—on the rare nights he slept. He also bought

That Irritating Slipper: A sleepless Howard Hughes complained about the revolving sign on a tiny casino, the Silver Slipper, outside his hotel window. So he bought the place. (Special Collections, UNLV Library)

Commenting on the failure of Howard Hughes's "seven Mormons up there in the penthouse" to exert much control over the casinos he had bought, writer Nicholas Pileggi says: "They never went down. They didn't know what was going on. In a lot of those casinos, skimming continued."

and completed a half-abandoned project, the Landmark, a round hotel-casino chiefly noted for its odd rooms, each shaped like a slice of pie.

During this same period, Hughes was buying a small airline, an airport, a motel, a restaurant, gold and silver mines scattered across the state, tracts of valuable undeveloped land along the Strip, about a hundred residential lots—and a television station.

The Movie Fan

"While nine floors below, beyond the blocked-out windows of his penthouse retreat, Las Vegas was alive with neon and non-stop action, the only light in [Hughes's] bedroom beamed from the overworked TV," Michael Drosnin wrote in *Citizen Hughes.*

Hank Greenspun, who owned both the *Las Vegas Sun* and television station KLAS, later recalled why he sold the station to Hughes: "He wanted the station open all night long, and he wanted certain pictures to be shown. Every night it was a call to my home or a call someplace else. 'Can't you keep it open an extra hour?' [he'd ask]. If Mr. Maheu wasn't calling me to put a certain picture on, then [Hughes aide] J. Richard Gray was asking me to do it. And then they asked me to put somebody to work who would be helpful in ascertaining what kind of pictures Mr. Hughes liked."

Finally, Greenspun asked one of the aides, "Why don't you buy the station, and run it any way you damn please?"

That simple solution appealed to Hughes, and he bought it—for $3,600,000. He then set up his own schedule for a program he called the "Swinging Shift"—three movies played back to back. All the movies were chosen with one specific viewer in mind: Howard Hughes. He often hesitated before making his final selections, so the station manager could not put out a reliable advance schedule.

And when the movies were announced in advance, Hughes often demanded last-minute substitutions.

Hughes kept up a steady stream of complaints to the staff of KLAS. He was disturbed by unexplained seconds of silence while the station's operators were looking for the next film or tape, and he was outraged by the fact that the commercials came on "at a sound level 10, 15, or even almost 20 decibels above the sound level of the preceding film or tape." And the lighting of his chosen movies also irritated him. "In the Bette Davis film 'Stolen Life' and in the RKO film 'Half Breed,' the screen was almost black throughout its entire area for long periods of time," he told attorney Dick Gray, ordering him to deal with this major problem immediately.

On a typical evening, he asked the manager to substitute *Las Vegas Story* and *Sealed Cargo* for two films he had previously chosen: *Gang War* and *Great Jewel Robbery*.

The manager, after going along patiently for many weeks, finally complained. Viewers were asking the station "why one movie is listed in TV *Guide* or the newspapers and a different one is shown," he told Hughes (through the aides). This could cause problems with advertisers, too, the manager said. Hughes apologized, then came up with an easy solution. The station could stop magazine and newspaper listings of the titles of the three late-night movies, he suggested, then there would be no puzzled viewers.

"Bookmaker to the World"

Although he was now a dominant figure in Las Vegas casinos, Hughes was not satisfied. There were hundreds of millions of gamblers who would never get to Las Vegas.

"I told you once I was interested in acquiring one of the bookmaking establishments in town," he wrote to Maheu, recalling one

"Vegas when I knew it . . . was the most wonderful place in the world. When it was taken over by Hughes and all that it became a factory."
—Entertainer Rose Marie

of his early, modest plans for expansion. "Well, I don't see any point in buying just one of these books. It is my hope that the damnedest book operation anyone ever conceived can be developed."

He then outlined his plan. He would first set up a catalog listing "every man of substance, in the entirety of the U.S." and include "all the truly significant information necessary to appraise his ability to pay and his integrity."

Once Hughes had gathered that detailed information, then a wealthy man could telephone his team of bookmakers in Las Vegas from any place in the world and place a bet "on just about anything—a horse race at Hollywood Park, a track meet in Florida, a football game in New York, an election . . . the passage of some bill up in Congress—just about anything."

He then explained why he was certain "this kind of play would catch on": "Because men, simply by nature, like to show off. I can just see some minor league V.I.P. out to dinner with some very attractive young protagonist of the opposite sex, and he picks up the phone, brought to his table at Twenty-One, and he makes a five or ten thousand dollar bet over the phone.

"Then he turns to his girl and says: 'Well, I just won ten thousand in Vegas—Let's spend it!'"

Periodically Hughes would reread the memo he had prepared describing his thoughts of becoming "bookie to the entire world" and wonder why his aides never took the necessary steps to get it under way. It was one of the hundreds of great plans that his overworked aides never found time to put into practice.

Abandoned Dreams

Hughes began sketching out plans to reshape the town. He talked of building the largest hotel-casino in the world (with four thou-

sand rooms) and constructing a luxurious new international airport, then selling it to the town at cost. He considered buying three or four more casinos in Las Vegas and also Bill Harrah's enormously profitable casinos in Reno and at Lake Tahoe. He invested twenty million dollars in dozens of Nevada mining claims (most of which were later found to be worthless). He offered to underwrite a new medical school and to finance a foundation to plan for the entire future of Nevada. He also donated money to start the state's community college system.

Howard Hughes's Folly: The Landmark Hotel lost money from its beginnings in the 1960s. Having changed hands several times, it was $35 million in debt when it was demolished on November 7, 1995. (Special Collections, UNLV Library)

Then, on Tuesday, April 16, 1968, he read a news story that changed all his plans. Announcing that a massive hydrogen bomb—one hundred times more powerful than the atomic bomb dropped on Hiroshima—would be detonated in ten days, the reporter then observed: "Persons up to about 250 miles from the detonation may feel a slight earth tremor following the explosion, particularly if they are on upper floors of high buildings or other tall structures."

Hughes, hidden away on the top floor of the Desert Inn—less than a hundred miles from ground zero—saw this as a personal warning, and his reaction struck some of his aides as hysterical. He wrote to Maheu: "Bob, my future plans are in a state of complete chaos, as a result of what is happening."

He had been deeply concerned about the nearby bomb tests for many months and thought he had devised the right way to end them. He made elaborate plans to bribe three major political figures he believed had the power to call off all future activity at the testing range: President Lyndon B. Johnson, Democratic presidential candidate Hubert H. Humphrey, and Republican presidential candidate Richard M. Nixon.

Hughes's private secretary, Nadine Hensley, recalled that Bob Maheu told her: "Mr. Hughes has approved $100,000 for each presidential candidate—$100,000 for Mr. Humphrey and $100,000 for Mr. Nixon."

Maheu later said that Hughes had decided also to promise retiring President Lyndon B. Johnson "a million dollars, after he left the office of the presidency, if he would stop the atomic testing before he left office." Maheu actually flew to Texas to meet with Johnson at his ranch to pass along that offer but could not bring himself to deliver Hughes's message. He knew Johnson would recognize this as a naked bribe.

Both Nixon and Humphrey accepted the cash gifts, according to Hughes aides, but did nothing to stop the feared tests.

In the months that followed, Hughes began looking for an alternate place to live. He told Maheu that there were too many things that disturbed him in Nevada. In addition to the bombs that terrified him, there were "a mass of miscellaneous problems which mainly seem to be a product of sharing the state with a number of other people. In other words, the unions, the minorities, the threat of overabundant competition."

In *Empire: The Life, Legend and Madness of Howard Hughes,* Donald L. Bartlett and James B. Steele describe Hughes's sudden departure from the town he had once hoped to reshape and dominate: "On Thanksgiving Eve, four years after his arrival in Las Vegas, Howard Hughes—just recovering from an attack of pneumonia—was placed on a stretcher, carried out of the Desert Inn unnoticed to a waiting van, and driven to Nellis Air Force Base, where a Lockheed JetStar was waiting . . . to fly him to the Bahamas. Nobody noticed. On Thanksgiving Day, the drapes remained tightly drawn across the Desert Inn penthouse windows and life went on as it had when the state's largest private employer and landowner was in residence."

Nearly a week went by without any public notice of his departure. Then, on December 2, 1970, Hank Greenspun published an Extra edition of the *Las Vegas Sun* with two startling headlines spread across the front page: HOWARD HUGHES VANISHES! MYSTERY BAFFLES CLOSE ASSOCIATES.

Greenspun's story began: "Howard Hughes, often called the phantom financier since he established permanent residence in Las Vegas in 1966, is involved in a disappearance from Nevada under circumstances even more mysterious than his secrecy-shrouded arrival. He was spirited away from the Desert Inn the evening of

"I think that towards the end of his stay [in Las Vegas] that some of his demands were not reasonable," Hughes aide Robert Maheu commented. "Unfortunately, I was not aware at that time the extent to which he was dependent on drugs. . . . I knew he had an entourage that was encouraging his lack of decision because it made them more powerful. But I thought I could control it as long as he and I could talk but I did not make arrangements—stupidly on my part—for the day he was too sick to communicate with me. And that's exactly what happened. . . . At that point I was fired. I was the last window to the world that Hughes had."

Movies on Demand: When Howard Hughes wanted to see a certain movie, usually late at night, he'd call Hank Greenspun, owner of the *Las Vegas Sun* and TV station KLAS. Greenspun sold Hughes the station and said, "Run it any way you damn please." (*Las Vegas Sun*)

"He loved to have maps that showed what Las Vegas was like in 1960 and he could see where the growth was going," Robert Maheu recalled. "At times he would say to me because I had to go somewhere to represent him, 'How I wish I could have been there.' And I'd say, 'Howard, damn it, do it.' And he'd say, 'I can't get myself to do that.' At the completion of these conversations I'd come back and my wife would say, 'A long conversation, honey?' And I'd say, 'With the poorest man in the world.'"

November 25 and even his top aides profess no knowledge of his whereabouts."

The Hughes era had ended. He would spend his last years moving restlessly from the Britannia Beach Hotel in the Bahamas to the Intercontinental Managua in Nicaragua, on to the Inn on the Park in London, from there to the Xanadu Princess Hotel on Grand Bahama Island, and then to the penthouse of the Acapulco Princess Hotel in Mexico.

In April 1976, he left Acapulco on his final journey. "The jet carrying Howard Hughes from Mexico on April 5, 1976, touched down at Houston International Airport at 1:50 P.M.," biographers Bartlett and Steele write. "Orderlies lifted his body out of the cabin and placed it in a green and white ambulance for the drive to the Methodist Hospital, twenty-eight miles to the south. . . .

"The ambulance came to a stop at a rear dock of [the hospital] at 2:50 P.M. and Hughes was carried to the morgue in the basement."

Howard Hughes was buried less than forty-eight hours later, at an eight-minute service attended by a few distant relatives. The dean of the church Hughes had attended as a child quoted from the *Book of Common Prayer:* "We brought nothing into the world and it is certain we will take nothing out."

Others had already begun reshaping the playground Howard Hughes had dominated for four years.

Music Makers: They wrote the song for another singer, but Mike Stoller (left) and Jerry Leiber (right) climbed to the top of the pop music charts when Elvis Presley recorded "Hound Dog." (MGM publicity photo)

10

THE ENTERTAINERS

"Elvis . . . who?"

That April night in 1956, the audience in the Venus Room at the New Frontier had come to laugh with comedian Shecky Greene, to hear familiar tunes played by Freddy Martin and his orchestra. So where did the management find this cotton-mouth rock-'n'-roll singer? Elvis Presley? Outside the casino there was a twenty-four-foot-tall cardboard figure of Elvis with a guitar. Posters called him "The Atomic Powered Singer," but most of these Las Vegas show-goers had never heard of him.

Their teenage children and grandchildren could have told them plenty. Back home in Memphis, Elvis had been mobbed by fans since he was a high school boy with his first record, "That's All Right, Mama." And when he went on tour with a radio show, *Louisiana Hayride,* country music fans clamored for more. Then, under the direction of a wily manager who called himself Colonel Tom Parker, Elvis had become a rock-'n'-roll recording star. His "Heartbreak Hotel" was number one on the pop charts.

The Colonel was confident that Las Vegas was waiting to embrace his popular client, but fans of Frank Sinatra, Dean Martin, and Liberace were not impressed. Local critics yawned. *Variety* said "Elvis Presley . . . doesn't hit the mark here." *Newsweek* compared Presley's Las Vegas debut to "a jug of corn liquor at a champagne party."

Trading places for a rare photo together, Liberace borrowed Elvis Presley's guitar, and the rock singer rippled the keyboard of the showman's very grand piano. (Las Vegas News Bureau)

In spite of the lukewarm reception, Elvis completed his two-week engagement in Las Vegas—two twelve-minute shows a night for fourteen nights and a special Saturday matinee for teen fans. With plenty of free time to explore the town, Elvis and his buddies looked for carnival rides, movies, and girls. Elvis didn't gamble, but the Colonel encouraged him to see other casino shows, to find out what the Las Vegas headliners were doing. That's when Elvis met Liberace, the Wisconsin-born pianist whose swooning audiences were packing the showroom at the Riviera. Publicity photos taken at that meeting were circulated everywhere and were still surfacing forty years later.

Shecky Greene was the popular headliner at the New Frontier when Elvis made his Las Vegas debut as a back-up act, "The Atomic Powered Singer." (Las Vegas News Bureau)

A lounge act at the Sands, Freddie Bell and the Bellboys, was such a hit with Elvis that he kept going back to see it again and again. What he liked best was Bell's showstopper song that began, "You ain't nuthin' but a hound dog!" Elvis loved it and learned it. In *Last Train to Memphis*, Peter Guralnick's almost day-by-day biography of Elvis Presley, the author says the song had already been a huge success in 1953 for a black singer, Big Mama Thornton.

"Hound Dog," Guralnick wrote, "had been written by two white teenagers, Jerry Leiber and Mike Stoller, who specialized in rhythm and blues, and was a very odd choice for a male performer, since it was written from a female point of view." Nevertheless, the song became Elvis's next big hit.

In June he sang "Hound Dog" on Milton Berle's television show. Elvis was a sensation, but his controversial gyrating performance stirred so much talk that the mayor of Jersey City, New Jersey, banned rock-'n'-roll from the city limits. Elvis's name became a household word to spark family arguments. His face, licensed by the Colonel, appeared on charm bracelets and decorated lipsticks in "Hound Dog Orange."

That summer, Elvis went to Hollywood to make his first movie, *Love Me Tender*. By the time it was released, the Elvis face had appeared on the covers of a dozen magazines and was familiar even to blue-haired grandmothers who had rejected him in Las Vegas. When Elvis was drafted into the Army in 1958, the whole world seemed to know who he was. Reporters chronicled his basic training and overseas service, keeping track of the RCA record sales that were making the singer a millionaire in his absence.

The next time Las Vegas saw Elvis Presley, he was a movie star, back in town with dancer/actress Ann-Margret in 1963 to film *Viva Las Vegas*. Traveling with an entourage of old friends, nicknamed "the Memphis Mafia," Elvis was mobbed by crowds of teenage girls everywhere he went. His escapades with young girls were notorious, but fan magazines reported a romance with his co-star. Meanwhile, a Texas teenager he had met in Germany, Priscilla Beaulieu, was waiting for him at Graceland, the lavish Memphis mansion Elvis had built for his mother before she died.

The Las Vegas wedding of Elvis and Priscilla Presley made entertainment news in 1967. By that time, Elvis had been replaced at the top of the recording charts by a British singing group, the Beatles. But Vegas was different. In Vegas, Elvis became King. By 1969 he was the star attraction at Kirk Kerkorian's brand-new International Hotel (now the Las Vegas Hilton). Night after night, Elvis performed for capacity crowds in the two-thousand-seat showroom, the largest in Las Vegas at the time. The hotel built a penthouse for him on its thirtieth floor, and Elvis lived there with his friends when he was in town.

The King's Final Years

Marty Lacker, "foreman of the Memphis Mafia," later recalled some of the financial details: "The deal the Colonel struck with the ho-

tel, was that Elvis would play two shows a day, seven days a week, for a month. . . . And for that he got $100,000 a week, or $400,000 for the month."

Another faithful member of the entourage, Lamar Fike, remembered how hard Elvis worked for the money: "Do you realize what kind of hell four weeks is? That's a marathon—nearly sixty performances. And Elvis had such a high-energy show that when he would do an honest hour and fifteen minutes twice a night, he was so tired he was cross-eyed. That's why he took all that stuff to keep him going."

Caught up in the fast life of Las Vegas entertainment, Elvis became infamous for his excesses. Photographs taken in 1976 show him bloated and unsmiling. In August 1977, less than ten years after his opening at the International, Elvis was dead—drug-ridden and exhausted at forty-two.

In Las Vegas, long after his death, dozens of Elvis impersonators kept his memory alive. Tourists found the Elvis Elvis Elvis Museum of Elvis Mementos, until it closed in the early 1990s. A few

"Elvis was destined to return to Las Vegas again and again . . . falling into one of those treadmill patterns that characterized his entire career. Every August and February, like clockwork, Colonel Parker would throw a switch and the machine would spring into action."—Albert Goldman, *Elvis*

old-timers remembered his first appearance at the New Frontier in 1956. Some of them talked about it during a four-hour television documentary about Las Vegas shown on the Arts and Entertainment Network in December 1996: "I tell you, one of the nicest people I've ever worked with in my life was Elvis Presley," Shecky Greene recalled forty years after Elvis appeared as a supporting act for his comedy show. "All the other stuff that I heard about him later on, I don't want to hear about it. You know, I just want to remember that nice kid."

"He was such a nice, clean young man," said singer Kay Starr, "and the Colonel was trying to tell me what all he did, and I couldn't feature this nice kid that looked like he just stepped out of the choir doing all those things."

A Time to Remember

"[Jack] Entratter, a former bouncer at the Copa, was revered by show biz performers. He was the first of the Vegas impresarios to understand that 'superstars' in a show room meant full houses, which in turn meant packed casinos before and after the show. He also understood that performers wanted to be treated like royalty, that they needed to be wined and dined and taken care of. Entratter did that, and the biggest stars of the 1950s and early 1960s all played the Sands."—Jefferson Graham, *Vegas: Live and In Person*

In the 1950s and 1960s, Las Vegas entertainment meant big-name stars, lavish costumes, extravagant salaries. Some entertainers, like Elvis, were destroyed by it. Others survived to remember it fondly.

"The money was enormous," comedian Red Buttons recalled on the 1996 television documentary. "Four weeks in Vegas could buy you a Third World country."

Singer Wayne Newton remembered the camaraderie. "I loved it when Elvis was at the Hilton and Sammy was at the Sands and Frank was at Caesars and Dean was at the Riv. The greatest entertainers in the world, bar none—and we were all friends!"

Newton, a Las Vegas showroom regular since his Downtown debut at the age of fifteen, was a relative newcomer to the Strip in the sixties. Sammy Davis Jr. had been singing, dancing, and clowning on Las Vegas stages for years. Frank Sinatra, idol of teenage girls in the 1940s, had been a star attraction at the Desert Inn and the Sands in the 1950s, long before Caesars opened in 1966. Dean Martin, after a series of movie roles as straight man opposite comedian Jerry Lewis, was building his Las Vegas reputation as a romantic singer. Separately, these veteran performers drew crowds to the casinos. When some of them started appearing together in 1960, they were dynamite.

"The event that put Vegas on the front page of every newspaper throughout the world was the Summit," said producer George Schlatter, once entertainment director at the New Frontier, "when Dean, Frank, Joey Bishop, Sammy Davis and Peter Lawford were on stage at the same time at the Sands."

Schlatter may have overstated the newspaper coverage, but the effect of this team on Las Vegas was electric. Earlier, the five had been friends, hanging out backstage at each other's shows, referring to themselves as "the Clan." The press called them "the Rat Pack." They preferred Sinatra's title for the group, "the Summit," and they called him "Chairman of the Board." In 1960 the five were making a movie together in Hollywood and Las Vegas.

The film was *Ocean's Eleven,* a comedy about a plot to rob five Las Vegas casinos. Since the actors were working together on the movie set every morning, Sinatra suggested a joint appearance in the Sands' Copa Room at night. In those days, the Copa Room was the place to be. Top performers like Milton Berle, Nat "King" Cole, and Danny Thomas had been headliners in the Copa Room since its opening in 1952, but Sinatra drew the biggest crowds. He was also part owner of the casino.

When Sinatra's Rat Pack took over the stage—singing, bantering, ad-libbing, and mingling with the crowds—the room was jammed with celebrities. Not only entertainers. These fans included politicians and jet-setting socialites. When Senator John F. Kennedy, campaigning for the presidency, was in Las Vegas to meet with Nevada delegates, the young Democratic candidate turned up at the Sands to see his brother-in-law, Peter Lawford, cavort with

About the "Rat Pack": "They would work all day on the picture (*Ocean's Eleven*) then go in the steam room, come outta the show, do the show on stage (where they had an occasional beverage, as you may remember). And then they, like, fainted between shows. Then they went out and did a second show and then took a nap and got ready to go out to the set of the movie at 6 the next morning."—Show producer George Schlatter

The Rat Pack—Peter Lawford, Frank Sinatra, Dean Martin, Sammy Davis, and Joey Bishop—held court often, clowning on stage in the Sands showroom. (Las Vegas News Bureau)

Sinatra and friends. After the show, Kennedy joined the performers for an informal celebration.

"Frank had been getting the theatrical community behind Kennedy," Sammy Davis reported in *Why Me? The Sammy Davis, Jr., Story* (with Jane and Burt Boyar), "and the five of us had been doing rallies and campaigning for him." After his inauguration, Kennedy came back to Las Vegas from time to time. When he did, news cameras clicked all night long.

The Sands had just one star dressing room, and the Rat Pack shared it. Davis remembered one night when Sinatra came in, just before the second show, and told them JFK was going to be out front.

"We always had celebrities in the audience," Davis said. "All five of us were onstage and we'd introduce them round-robin, each of us taking one, always saving the biggest for last. . . . That night Frank stepped back to where we had a bar on the stage and as I was pouring a drink he said, 'Smokey, you introduce the President.' Frank threw that to me! Instead of taking the glory for himself and doing a number with it—which *I* would have done if I'd been that close to the man—he gave it to *me*."

The two entertainers had been friends long before the others entered the picture, and Davis had been in show business the longest of all. As a child he had performed in New York and across the country with his father in "Will Mastin's Gang, featuring Little Sammy." Later, their act became the popular Will Mastin Trio.

"My home has always been show business," Davis recalled in *Why Me?* "That's where I've lived since the age of three. I've slept in hotels and rooming houses, in cars, on trains and buses, in our dressing rooms, with my father and a man I called my uncle, Will Mastin; and, when we were out of work, with my grandmother, Rosa B. Davis, whom I called Mamma, at her place in Harlem. But home was where the lights were, the people out front, the laughter and applause, the acts that I watched from the wings all day long. . . . I had traveled ten states and played over fifty cities by the time I was four."

Audiences cheered his song and dance performances and later his impersonations of famous entertainers. He met Sinatra in Detroit in 1940 when the singer and the Will Mastin Trio were on the same bill with Tommy Dorsey's orchestra. Five years later, after Davis returned from military duty in Army Special Services, they met again in Los Angeles, where armies of screaming teenagers in bobby socks waited for Sinatra at the stage door. Davis joined the fans, asked for Sinatra's autograph, and the singer remembered him. From that time on, Sinatra and Davis kept in touch. Sometimes they found themselves in Las Vegas at the same time.

"Those shows were just a lot of fun. . . . It was like the air sparkled with electricity! And everybody flew in from all over the world."—Former Copa dancer Jeannie Gardner

The Strip and the Ghetto

With the Will Mastin Trio, Sammy Davis Jr. made his Las Vegas debut in 1945 at El Rancho Vegas on Highway 91. Within a few years,

The Will Mastin Trio with Sammy Davis Jr. was a hit at the El Rancho Vegas in 1945, but black entertainers had to find rooms on the other side of town. (Las Vegas News Bureau)

that stretch of highway would become the famous Las Vegas Strip, studded with casinos and entertainers, but in the early 1940s the El Rancho was a pioneer, offering big-name entertainers from Hollywood. A mile down the road, the Last Frontier was its only competition. Davis and his costars were ecstatic to be offered $500 a week at El Rancho.

"The band was the biggest we'd ever worked with," Davis recalled. "The floor of the stage was springy; the lighting was the most modern I'd ever seen. After rehearsal we asked about our rooms. The manager said, 'We can't let you have rooms here. You'll have to find a place on the other side of town.' " It was a slap in the face. For the rest of his life, Sammy Davis would remember his introduction to the ugly face of racial prejudice in Las Vegas. Over the years, he would see more of it.

"No performer has been playing the city as long [as Davis]," Jefferson Graham wrote in *Vegas: Live and In Person,* his 1989 illustrated portrait of the city. "No white performer has suffered the indignities Davis endured playing Vegas in the 1940s and 1950s."

Davis summed up the experience: "We were performing at the hotel, but we couldn't stay there. We couldn't eat there. We couldn't gamble in the casino. We couldn't walk in the front door." Other black entertainers—Ella Fitzgerald, Pearl Bailey, Lena Horne, Billy Eckstine, Harry Belafonte, and Nat "King" Cole—also found themselves barred from the hotels.

"In Vegas, for twenty minutes, our skin had no color," Davis recalled. "Then, the second we stepped off the stage, we were colored again. . . . The other acts could gamble or sit in the lounge and have a drink, but we had to leave through the kitchen with the garbage. I was dying to grab a look into the casino, just to see what it was like, but I was damned if I would let anyone see me with my nose against the candy-store window."

Morton Saiger, a Polish immigrant who worked at the Last Frontier in the 1940s, remembered those days in an oral history for the University of Nevada: "Many black entertainers worked at the Last Frontier but could not stay there. It was unfortunate, but that was the law. I was so hurt that I couldn't see straight because this was the way I was treated in Poland as a Jew, so I just ached. . . . If we had some black entertainers, I had to pick them up at six to bring them down to the show. We had rooming houses in the West Side, which was known as the colored neighborhood at the time. . . . I had to take them back after midnight, because there was no other transportation over to the West Side."

Saiger recalled a performance by Sammy Davis at the Last Frontier, before he became a solo act: "The Will Mastin Trio were through about ten, and at twelve they had to go on again. They

"Las Vegas needed a place where all blacks could go. Efforts to provide black soldiers and tourists with an interracial hotel-casino date from 1942 when the Horace Heidt Corporation attempted to open the Shamrock Hotel downtown. Protests from nearby whites combined with the city's emerging Jim Crow policy to deny the hotel an operating permit. This move resulted in an organized march on City Hall by several hundred blacks, but town fathers were adamant."
—Eugene Moehring, *Resort City in the Sunbelt*

couldn't even eat in the kitchen. There was a picnic table outside the kitchen. I had to bring out sandwiches for them to eat there."

Race relations in Las Vegas didn't get much better in the 1950s. *Ebony* magazine reported in 1951 that Las Vegas lagged far behind other cities in civil rights, with the exception of the Deep South. Nevada was called "Mississippi of the West." In that uncomfortable climate, a group of entrepreneurs opened the first integrated hotel-casino in Las Vegas.

West Side Showplace

When the Moulin Rouge opened its doors on West Bonanza Avenue in May 1955, it was a glittering showplace. Mahogany-lined walls, crystal chandeliers, generous swimming pool, and spacious showroom made it a serious competitor for gamblers and show-goers who filled the five big hotel-casinos on the other side of town. Famous black entertainers were brought in from all over the world and black tourists filled the hotel. Every night, after their performances at other casinos, black and white entertainers came to the Moulin Rouge for late-night jam sessions. Showroom crowds followed them to the West Side.

The Moulin Rouge, the first racially integrated casino in Las Vegas, opened in May 1955, attracted crowds of celebrities—black and white—but its success was short lived. (Special Collections, UNLV Library)

"If Las Vegas had been a southern town, the opening of the Moulin Rouge might be considered by some to be the beginning of the civil rights movement," says a character in *Death of a Tenor Man*, a 1995 suspense novel by jazz musician and writer Bill Moody. The murder mystery pursued in Moody's novel is fictional, but the vivid background is based on fact, records preserved in newspaper files and in the library at the University of Nevada, Las Vegas, where Moody has taught English. Opening night at the Moulin Rouge is presented by Moody as described in a forty-year-old diary kept by one of his fictional showgirls: "They just kept coming in big limos—

Harry Belafonte, Sammy Davis and the man, Nat King Cole!!!!—dressed so fine, and there were photographers everywhere, even some people from *Life* magazine."

A photo of actual showgirls on the cover of *Life* magazine and more photos inside the magazine record the Moulin Rouge opening for history. For the next few months, the place filled with celebrities. Then suddenly, without explanation, it closed in September. Why? There was speculation that the Moulin Rouge had lured business away from other casinos and that the owners were pressured by Mob interests to remove the unwanted competition. Whatever the reason, the place was sold and never quite regained its early glory—in spite of efforts by a long list of subsequent owners.

Fewer than ten years after its 1955 opening, the Moulin Rouge had become a meeting place for community leaders, black and white, seeking an end to segregation in Las Vegas. When members of the NAACP met at the Moulin Rouge with Governor Grant Sawyer and the Nevada Resort Association in 1960, they reached an agreement that led eventually to the desegregation of the Strip.

Slowly, the situation began to improve as the Civil Rights movement gained momentum. In his own corner of the movement, Sammy Davis Jr. kept chipping away at barriers. When the Will Mastin Trio moved from the Last Frontier to the Sands in 1958, Davis went to entertainment director Jack Entratter and said he and his father and uncle had to be allowed to live at the Sands while performing there. Entratter moved the trio into the hotel, but registration still wasn't open to everybody. As late as 1961, African Americans were still having a hard time getting through the front door at the Sands.

According to Jefferson Graham: "Davis was sitting with Frank Sinatra in the lobby one afternoon when a black couple walked in the front door and two security guards walked over to block them. . . . Davis and Sinatra walked over to the guards and . . . the unofficial president of the hotel told the guards that the couple were his guests and ushered them in. Then Sinatra called Sands executive Carl Cohen on the phone."

Sinatra's colorful language evidently made an impression. "The next day," Graham reports, "Davis went to Entratter and suggested that now was the time to start hiring blacks at the Sands. . . . The entertainer went to the NAACP, which sent over a group of applicants; suddenly the Sands was hiring black bellhops, busboys and waiters." The doors were swinging open.

Chairman of the Board

"If one individual could be said to embody the high-low spirit of Las Vegas," British author David Spanier wrote in 1987, "it is Frank Sinatra. For three decades he has made it his kind of town. No other cabaret performer packs in the audiences he does. When

Sinatra comes to town, everybody lives it up. . . . He is a man who lives gambling, who likes to play high, who mingles with the big boys behind the scenes, and has made no secret of the fact that he owns part of their action and they own part of him. . . . Vegas has taken him to its neon heart."

In *Inside the Gambler's Mind*, Spanier borrows a 1985 "Doonesbury" cartoon strip to illustrate his view of Sinatra: At a casino gaming table, an invisible Sinatra is firing a fusillade of deleted expletives at the dealer, ordering her not to shuffle the cards. The law-abiding dealer apologizes politely but says she must follow the house rules. When a pit boss arrives to settle the dispute, he reprimands the dealer: "What's the matter with you, girl! Frank Sinatra is ABOVE the rules! He's ABOVE simple courtesy! He does it his way!"

Sinatra's friends are loyal. Countless showbiz biographies document his generosity and tireless capacity for work, but even his friends attest to his contempt for any rules during the Rat Pack years and his tendency to get into fights with reporters, photographers, waiters, and anybody else who dared to defy his wishes. His rumored ties to organized crime led to intensive questioning by federal investigators and eventual loss of some of his casino interests, but many media reports continued to view those ties with a mixture of indulgence and admiration. Sinatra had staying power. More than half a century after his voice first charmed radio listeners in the 1940s, Sinatra was part of the Las Vegas legend, and when he died in 1998, the lights of the brightest city in the world were dimmed in his honor.

"Mister Showmanship"

There was a time when the undisputed monarch of Las Vegas was a flamboyant pianist whose fingers rippled over the keys of a rhinestone-studded Baldwin piano at the Riviera. Liberace was the hot-

"Probably the most celebrated example of the Las Vegas/Hollywood connection is the Frank Sinatra case. Affiliated with a gambling operation in Las Vegas and Lake Tahoe casinos in the 1950s, Sinatra had his gambling license revoked in 1963 during the 'hang tough' days of Governor Sawyer because he allegedly maintained contacts in his casino operations with an underworld figure who was on the state's black list. He engaged in a bitter exchange of accusations with the state's gambling control officials."—James W. Hulse, *Forty Years in the Wilderness*

test star of the moment in 1953 when the brand-new Riviera paid him an unheard-of fifty thousand dollars a week to leave the Last Frontier, where he had been under contract since 1946. Publicity shots of his extravagant costumes—decorated with sequins, ostrich feathers, and bugle beads—were published worldwide. Press photographers jostled each other in the showroom, night after night, to capture on film Liberace's latest full-length fur cape.

Middle-aged women in his audiences squealed like teenagers when he swept onstage, flashed a dimpled smile, and seated himself at the piano. Soft light from an ornate silver candelabra, his trademark, set the mood as he played romantic favorites, from light classics to popular hits. Some fans wore miniature candelabra pins. Across the country, more fans waited for and watched Liberace's television broadcasts on 184 channels.

Before becoming an entertainment legend, young Liberace had been a prodigy pianist at age seven in his native Wisconsin and a concert performer at fourteen. He was one of a pair of twins born in 1919 to Frances Zuchowski Liberace and her husband Salvatore. One twin died at birth, and the parish priest in Milwaukee christened the survivor Wladziu Valentino Liberace, reflecting his mother's Polish heritage and his father's Italian origins. On the baby's birth certificate, the name was Americanized as *Walter* Valentino Liberace—the name the pianist used until 1950, when he had it legally changed to simply "Liberace." Family and friends called him "Lee."

As a performer, Liberace cringed when anyone mispronounced his name, especially if he were introduced as "Mr. Lib-er-ACE," rhyming with "trace." So he started sending out handwritten postcards to talent buyers and press people, announcing his current engagement above a flowing signature, "Liberace (libber-AH-chee)."

In his 1987 biography *Liberace,* veteran Hollywood newsman and

Flamboyant Liberace, with his rhinestone-studded Baldwin piano, silver candelabra, and ornate costumes, lived in Las Vegas, where he was a showroom star for forty years. (Las Vegas News Bureau)

author Bob Thomas illustrates the pianist's life story with dozens of revealing anecdotes. One story recalls Liberace's first rehearsal in the Ramona Room of the Last Frontier: "The showroom's facilities were primitive," Thomas writes, "and . . . he could find no one to assist him. Finally he spotted a tall, skinny man standing by the light switchboard.

"'Oh, hi there,' Liberace began. 'Now here's my sheet of light cues. Basically, I want blues, pinks and magentas when I'm doing a soft number. Then when I pick up the beat, bring up the color—lots of reds and whites. If I play *Claire de Lune,* be sure to give me a blue light. Y'understand?'

"The man nodded as [entertainment director] Maxine Lewis approached and remarked, 'Oh, I didn't realize you knew Howard Hughes.'"

From the Last Frontier to the Riviera to the Hilton and Caesars Palace, Liberace spent the next forty years performing regularly in Las Vegas. Even when he toured the world, entertaining crowds in London, Paris, or Sydney, he was "Mister Las Vegas." The Nevada city was his legal residence when he died in 1987. At a Las Vegas memorial service in St. Anne's Roman Catholic Church, three priests conducted a mass, Robert Goulet delivered the eulogy, and stars and stagehands mingled with Liberace fans while the organ played his familiar sign-off song, "I'll Be Seeing You."

Ten years after his death, the Liberace Museum on East Tropicana Avenue was still a tourist attraction so successful that it ranked ahead of everything else in the area—except the casinos, Hoover Dam, and Lake Mead. Long before the museum opened in 1979, Liberace had offered to build one in Milwaukee to house his treasures—costumes, jewelry, pianos, automobiles, and miniature collections—but his birth city declined. So Liberace built his museum in Las Vegas and became a hometown boy.

Nostalgic fans still buy tickets to see and hear "Liberace"—along with impersonators of Elvis Presley, Marilyn Monroe, Louie Armstrong, and other dead stars—in "Legends in Concert," a long-running show at the Imperial Palace.

"King of the Strip"

Whenever a star disappears from the Las Vegas scene, a dozen more performers are waiting in the wings, ready to step into the spotlight. Wayne Newton didn't wait. He claimed his Las Vegas spotlight in 1959, when he was just fifteen, and kept on moving up to bigger and brighter marquees. In the 1990s he was called "King of the Strip" and "The Midnight Idol." For some audiences he succeeded Liberace as "Mister Las Vegas."

Like Liberace and Sammy Davis Jr., Newton started performing as a child. He was only six when he and his brother, Jerry, started

Wayne Newton was just fifteen in 1959 when he first sang at the Fremont Hotel in Downtown Las Vegas. Over the years he became a one-man variety show and is still a headliner in the nineties. (Las Vegas News Bureau)

singing together publicly in Roanoke, Virginia. When their family moved to Phoenix, Arizona, the brothers were hired to appear on a local daily television show. Their popularity led to a five-year contract in the Carnival Lounge at the Fremont Hotel in Downtown Las Vegas. Too young to enter casinos alone without breaking Nevada gaming laws, the boys had to be escorted into the lounge every night.

Years later, Wayne told a reporter he was disappointed in Las Vegas at first. Expecting to find a fantasyland, he discovered that "it was just a matter of plopping down and going to work and falling into the routine of doing six shows a night."

When Wayne got a recording contract in 1963 and scored big hits with "Red Roses for a Blue Lady" and "Danke Schön," he was given top billing. The Newton Brothers became "Wayne Newton with Jerry Newton." For a few more years, Jerry played guitar and straight man for his brother's jokes then left for Tennessee. Wayne moved from Downtown to the Strip and never left. As a headliner at the Flamingo, the Frontier, Las Vegas Hilton, and his own Aladdin, Newton became a one-man variety show.

Late in the 1990s, Newton is still a headliner, playing guitar, banjo, and a lightning-fast fiddle, doing two hours of show tunes and old favorites, from "Danke Schön" to "When the Saints Go Marching In," at each performance. When his name goes up on a marquee at the MGM Grand, fans still line up for tickets. Offstage, he lives just outside the city on his ranch, Casa Shenandoah, where he keeps Arabian horses. Wayne Newton is at home in Las Vegas.

Magic Is In

When Siegfried Fischbacher and Roy Horn came to Las Vegas from the Lido de Paris in 1971, they were billed as a specialty act, deco-

Siegfried and Roy bring white tigers, bred in their animal sanctuary near Las Vegas, to wander in a Secret Garden at the Mirage. Show-goers fill Theatre Mirage every night when the two illusionists perform their magic. (Mirage Resorts)

rating several production shows around town with their smoothly choreographed illusions and disappearing acts. Ten years later they were ready for their own show. "Beyond Belief" became a hot ticket, and "Siegfried and Roy" didn't need last names any more. Now their faces, cast in bronze, gaze out from an eighteen-foot sculpture, unveiled in 1993, in front of Steve Wynn's Mirage.

Twice nightly, during three weeks of each month, the two magicians perform at the Mirage with their white Bengal tigers—but the tigers are not merely performers or props in a magic show. Since the 1980s, Siegfried and Roy have been active conservationists, working to protect and preserve endangered animals. White tigers, native to India, were almost extinct when the illusionists founded a "Living Classroom" breeding program with the Zoological Society of Cincinnati.

Starting with a white tiger cub and two striped white tigers, they nurtured a family of rare animals that grew into forty big cats they named the Royal White Tigers of Nevada. In 1994, Siegfried and Roy were asked by the South African government to set up a similar breeding program for lions—the endangered White Lions of Timbavati. At that time, specialists at the Johannesburg Zoological Gardens said there were no more white lions in the wild and only ten in captivity. Within three years, Siegfried and Roy had helped to increase that number to eighteen—and eleven of them lived in Las Vegas.

At the Mirage in 1997, the entertainers opened their Secret Garden where visitors could see endangered animals in a natural setting. Six rare breeds shared the garden in apparent harmony with each other. An Asian elephant, panthers, and a snow leopard joined the royal white tigers, the white lions of Timbavati, and a few striped heterozygous Bengal tigers.

Like Liberace and Wayne Newton, Siegfried and Roy have become permanent residents of Las Vegas.

"When we first started here, magic was always shoved to the back of the show," Siegfried told a reporter a few years ago. "It never went on the marquee. Now almost every major showroom has a magic act. . . . Magic is *in*."

Roy agrees. "If you want to be Pope you have to go to Rome, but if you want to make it in show business—in our style of show business—you have to go to Las Vegas."

Fantasy Man: Flamboyant Jay Sarno, creator of Caesars Palace and Circus Circus, made and lost several fortunes before he died in 1984. Whether he was planning a "Grandissimo" casino or eating two ice-cream cones at once, he believed in living on a grand scale. (Las Vegas News Bureau)

11

THREE TYCOONS

Jay Sarno, a gambler who had made a modest fortune from a string of cabana motor inns, was not impressed by the once-famous casinos he visited during his trips to Las Vegas in the late 1950s.

"The Flamingo was sick—like an old storage room," he said. "The Desert Inn was a stable." He observed that "Las Vegas had done the Wild Western motif to death. What it needed was a little true opulence."

Sarno decided to design an elaborate casino inspired by his conception of life under the Roman emperors and to call it Caesars Palace. (He deliberately omitted the apostrophe from Caesar's because that would mean the palace belonged to only one Caesar. "We wanted to create the feeling that everybody in the hotel was a Caesar," he said.)

The result was "the gaudiest, weirdest, most elaborate, and most talked about resort Vegas had ever seen," Jefferson Graham writes in *Vegas: Live and In Person*. "[Its] emblem was a chesty female dipping grapes into the waiting mouth of a recumbent Roman, fitted out in toga, laurel wreath, and phallic dagger."

Banks were not then ready to risk the nineteen million dollars or more Sarno and his partner, Nate Jacobsen, estimated they would need for this venture, so Jacobsen turned to Jimmy Hoffa and the Teamsters Union for most of the money. Because that was their chief source, rumors of Mob backing began circulating before Cae-

"Muzak pervades Las Vegas from the time you walk into the airport upon landing to the last time you leave the casinos. It is piped out to the swimming pool. It is in the drugstores. It is as if there were a communal fear that someone, somewhere in Las Vegas, was going to be left with a totally vacant minute on his hands."—Tom Wolfe, *Las Vegas (What?) Las Vegas (Can't hear you! Too noisy) Las Vegas!!!!*

sars opened, and Ovid Demaris, author of *The Boardwalk Jungle*, asserted flatly that Caesars Palace was "a mob-controlled casino from the day it opened its doors."

By August 5, 1966, Sarno and Jacobsen had spent twenty-five million dollars on Caesars and were ready for the opening. For this celebration they set aside another million. Guests ate two tons of filet mignon, drank fifty thousand glasses of champagne, and enjoyed "the largest order of Ukrainian caviar ever placed by a private organization."

Those who attended the opening were greeted by "long-legged Greco-Roman pony-tail-wigged cocktail waitresses, who were instructed to walk up . . . and say, 'Welcome to Caesars Palace, I am your slave,'" Jefferson Graham recalls.

Extraordinary publicity about the new showplace brought forty-two million dollars in advance bookings by the time the hotel-casino opened, and Caesars began to set new Las Vegas gambling records during its first week. For years it was the most profitable casino in the world.

The Man Behind Caesars

Jay Sarno may have been the first man to recognize exactly why people came to Las Vegas, said Alan Feldman, vice president of Mirage Resorts. "It wasn't the gambling that attracted people. It was the fantasy. He understood down to his shoes that they came here to get away from whatever it was at home, to lose themselves in Las Vegas.

"He knew that if the majority of people in the world could live like Caesar, they would live like Caesar."

Sarno himself did live like Caesar. His son, Jay C. Sarno, remembers his father once saying to a friend, "I'm going to make a million dollars this year. I can't live on that."

Caesars Palace, more than thirty years after it opened, is still an imperial presence on the Strip. It rises behind rows of towering fountains, stirring opulent fantasies for twenty-first-century visitors. (Las Vegas News Bureau)

During the good years, much of the elder Sarno's enormous income disappeared at the tables. The Sarnos were comped whenever they dined in Las Vegas, but almost always the elder Sarno fitted in a little gambling at the casino where they were eating.

Jay C. Sarno recalls one of his sisters saying one evening, "'It's nice that we get to eat free everywhere.' My mother looked at her and said, 'Your baked potato cost five thousand dollars.'"

The elder Sarno probably gambled away between twenty and twenty-five million dollars over his lifetime, young Sarno estimates. His extravagant manner of living was demonstrated by one other episode the family remembers. Sarno had owned a Cadillac about a year, and one day young Jay reminded him to have his oil changed. Sarno drove down to his dealer, saw a newer Cadillac on display that he liked better, and bought it. After that, his friends would say, "Jay changes the oil by changing the car."

"I am in the office of Major A. Riddle—Major is his name—the president of the Dunes hotel. . . . As everywhere else in Las Vegas, someone has turned on the air conditioning to the point where it will be remembered. . . . Riddle has an appointment to see a doctor at 4:30 about a crimp in his neck. His secretary, Maude McBride, has her head down and is rubbing the back of her neck. Lee Fisher, the P.R. man, and I are turning ours from time to time to keep the pivots from freezing up."—Tom Wolfe, *Las Vegas (What?) Las Vegas (Can't hear you! Too noisy) Las Vegas!!!!*

The Year-Round Circus

A restless man, Sarno was better at originating a concept such as Caesars than at running it. He sold Caesars Palace to the owners of the Lum's restaurant chain for sixty million dollars three years after the opening night.

Sarno's new idea was a casino surrounding the world's liveliest, most expensive, and most elaborate circus, which he gave the emphatic name Circus Circus.

Howard Hughes, who was hoping to make Las Vegas more attractive to wealthy, sophisticated gamblers from around the world, was appalled when he heard of Sarno's new project.

He sent one of his worried memos to his Las Vegas overseer, Bob Maheu: "The aspect of this circus that has me disturbed is the popcorn, peanuts, kids side of it. In other words, the poor, dirty shabby side of circus life. The dirty floor, sawdust and elephants. . . . After

Under the Big Top: Circus Circus today has expanded far beyond Jay Sarno's modest original into a resort covering sixty-nine acres. Beyond the parent resort, Circus Circus Enterprises encompasses Excalibur, Luxor, Monte Carlo (a joint venture with Mirage Resorts), the new Mandalay Bay, and more theme casinos in other cities. (Las Vegas News Bureau)

all, the Strip is supposed to be synonymous with a good looking female all dressed up in a very expensive diamond-studded evening gown and driving up to a multi-million-dollar hotel in a Rolls Royce."

Sarno astonished other critics by charging tourists admission to Circus Circus. (Las Vegans who could produce I.D. were admitted free.)

Potential visitors apparently shared Hughes's reservations about the pungent aroma in the new casino, and the number of gamblers who were ready to pay admission to any casino turned out to be limited. Circus Circus got off to a very slow start.

One other problem was a gregarious elephant who was taught by a trainer to pull the handle on a huge slot machine and to throw dice. "She would throw them halfway across the casino," young Sarno recalls. "Some gamblers didn't like that. It's noisy on the casino floor, and it's frightening when this big trunk comes past your shoulder and starts reaching out and bumping you."

Although he had come up with one of the most commercially valuable ideas in the history of Nevada casinos, Sarno soon lost much of the fortune he had made from Caesars Palace. In 1974 he sold Circus Circus to William G. Bennett, who neatened up the casino, quit charging admission, expanded the hotel, lowered prices, and "turned Circus Circus into low-roller heaven," Jefferson Graham writes.

Sarno could conceive of a place like Circus Circus and create it, Alan Feldman said, but he could not run it. What he needed was a skillful operating partner who would have asked him, "Jay, do you know what elephants *do*? They're not neat. Let's discuss this." Even after suffering disastrous losses, Sarno still had one other extravagant project in mind: the Grandissimo. He began looking for a backer with a billion dollars to help him construct the most

"The gambler at [Binion's] Horseshoe is allowed to set his own limit with his first bet. In 1980, for example, someone drove in off the desert carrying two suitcases, one empty, the other containing seven hundred and seventy-seven thousand dollars in hundred-dollar bills. He took the suitcases to the cage at the back of the casino and changed the neat packages of money into chips, and then, escorted by security guards, he carried his racked chips to a craps table, bet the lot on a single throw of the dice, won, returned to the cage with his double load of chips, filled both suitcases with money, and drove away. His only comment was, 'I reckoned inflation was going to eat that money up anyway, so I might as well double it or lose it all.' He has not been back."
—A. Alvarez, *The Biggest Game in Town*

luxurious hotel-resort in the world, with six thousand rooms. He planned a terraced end to one of the towers, which would have a waterfall cascading from the top down each floor. He also had an idea for a rollercoaster inside the casino.

"When he talked about anything like that, everybody would roll their eyes and say, 'What the hell kind of idea is that?'" young Sarno recalls. "Now it's becoming almost a standard component."

But he was shadowed by his failure in operating Circus Circus and died just as his money was running out in 1984, still dreaming of his most ambitious project.

Discovering Las Vegas

Kirk Kerkorian built his sixty-million-dollar hotel, the International, off the Strip on Paradise Road. In 1967 it was the world's biggest and most expensive hotel. Six years later it became the Las Vegas Hilton, but Kerkorian had even bigger plans. (Special Collections, UNLV Library)

During the first days of the Strip, a young pilot named Kirk Kerkorian flew gamblers from California to Las Vegas and sometimes stayed around to try his luck at the tables.

Son of an ambitious but unlucky Armenian fruit grower, Kerkorian had discovered by the time he was twenty that he had a natural talent for trading. He had also demonstrated his readiness to take risks, buying wartime surplus aircraft in Hawaii and flying the over-age planes to the United States, where he could sell each of them at a profit of ten to twelve thousand dollars—if he managed to complete the dangerous journey.

One of his early successes came from buying parts of two airplanes that had crashed, cutting away the sections that were damaged and creating a new, salable aircraft from the usable parts of the two wrecks.

After making fifty thousand dollars from buying and selling war surplus planes, Kerkorian took over a charter service that operated three second-hand aircraft. Then he began a lifelong custom of "trading up"—selling one enterprise for a substantial profit and immediately investing his sizable gains in a much more expensive project. He usually had the help of friendly bankers who were ready to join in each new gamble, impressed by his record of success.

At first his trades were in the thousands, then in the hundreds of thousands, then in the millions. After selling his interest in a small airline for eighty-five million dollars, he was ready to risk his fortune on a series of ambitious projects in Las Vegas.

New Millionaire in Town

Kerkorian began his major ventures in Nevada by buying the Flamingo, which had passed through many hands after the death of Bugsy Siegel. The casino was showing signs of age by 1968, and there were clear indications of major skimming by the previous owners.

Kerkorian found a manager who made the 767-room hotel and casino profitable, but his real interest was in using the Flamingo as a training place for the staff of a casino he had decided to build. This was the International—ambitiously planned as the largest, most expensive casino in the world. It was also the first one built on a Las Vegas "back street"—Paradise Road—rather than the Strip.

Kerkorian ran into problems borrowing sixty million dollars from the banks that had financed his earlier ventures. "I wore out two pair of shoes, pounding the pavement looking for financing," one of his assistants said after visiting major banks.

Howard Hughes, who was watching jealously from his Desert Inn hideaway, announced that he was ready to build a four-thousand-room Super Sands Hotel, with an indoor golf course, hoping that this would frighten his rival casino owner into abandoning his plans. Undisturbed, Kerkorian decided to go ahead with construction without waiting until he had all the money in hand, and his gamble on the 1,512-room giant paid off.

"The International turned one of the best profits in Las Vegas

> "Kirk Kerkorian was not cut out for the typical Hollywood celebrity scene. He has always driven his own car. He has never owned a Rolls-Royce. . . . [He] bought a Pontiac Firebird, the Pontiac version of the Mustang—the kind of car his secretaries could afford."
> —Kerkorian biographer Dial Torgerson

from the day it opened its doors," Dial Torgerson wrote in his biography of Kerkorian. "It brought in more than five million dollars during the first month."

Studio for Sale

The MGM film studios had some very difficult years in the 1960s, sometimes losing as much as thirty-five million dollars annually. But the corporation owned many acres of valuable real estate, an inventory of famous old films, a major record company, and other assets with an estimated resale value of $350,000,000.

Attracted by those half-hidden assets, Kerkorian bought controlling interest in MGM for about one-fourth of that estimated value. Then he hired James T. Aubrey Jr., the former president of CBS, to run the studio, which may have been his most serious mistake as an investor.

In New York, Aubrey had earned the nickname "The Smiling Cobra." He seemed to enjoy firing people and became famous for "wielding his charmed hatchet up and down Madison Avenue with the wildness and sureness of an Apache Indian," one television writer observed.

At first Aubrey concentrated on making films—and the results were often disastrous, both critically and commercially. As the losses grew, he began selling off many of the studio's assets, including *Gone with the Wind, Dr. Zhivago,* and other classic films. He also fired five out of every six employees, until both the offices and the backlots seemed deserted.

After four disastrous years, with one money-losing film following another in a monotonous sequence, Aubrey finally had "nothing left to do, nothing left to sell, and no one left to fire," Dial Torgerson observed. And then, one day, he too was gone.

Back to Las Vegas

Convinced that MGM was unlikely ever to regain its dominant position in Hollywood, Kerkorian turned his attention again to Las Vegas, hoping there to redeem the investment he had made in the studio. He decided once again to build the largest, most expensive casino in the world—and to call it MGM Grand, after the 1932 film classic *Grand Hotel*.

Not everyone was impressed by his idea. A writer in *Forbes* magazine commented: "It looks as though the old blue chip of the movie business is being cashed in for a stack of gambling chips."

Later, when the new direction of MGM came up for discussion at an annual meeting, one irate shareholder proclaimed loudly: "Mr. Kerkorian has the nerve not to show up, when the company's assets are being handed over to him." (Kerkorian is noted for skipping any meeting he does not have to attend—including many where he is expected to appear.)

The chairman responded calmly, but the shareholder was not appeased. "Where is Kerkorian?" she asked a few minutes later. "Is he in bed with a 104-degree fever? Why is he not here?"

"I suggest you ask him when you see him," the chairman replied softly, ignoring the fact that even Kerkorian's top executives could go for months without seeing him.

The cost of constructing the MGM Grand was first estimated at ninety million dollars. By the time the 2,100-room hotel-casino opened, expenditures had ballooned to $120,000,000. With 4,500 employees, the huge casino was extraordinarily expensive to operate, but in 1974 it earned back more than one-sixth of the investment: twenty-two million dollars. Even with MGM's near abandonment of movies, that year was the most profitable in the company's long history.

Disaster at Dawn

On November 21, 1980, the MGM Grand had an occupancy rate of 99 percent. At seven o'clock that morning, a waitress saw flames coming out of the keno board in the delicatessen. In *Welcome to the Pleasuredome,* David Spanier vividly describes the disaster that followed:

> Smoke is seen rising above the colossal front of the MGM. The alert is slow in coming. Inside the casino, crystal chandeliers crash down and ceiling panels crack and fall, while above, so far unseen by anyone, a second fireball races towards the front entrance. . . . Pipes, conduits and insulation material ignite and burn relentlessly. A moment after the wall of fire crashes

After the Fire: On November 21, 1980, Kerkorian saw his prized MGM Grand hotel consumed by fire. Pessimists thought this was the end for the hotel, but it reopened just eight months later. (Las Vegas News Bureau)

through the restaurant end of the casino, a second, more violent fire reaches the hotel's main entrance, dropping a blistering wall of flames that consumes everything in its path. . . . In just ninety seconds life ceased in the casino and surrounding areas. . . . As the fire roared through the casino, a cloud of toxic smoke poured up through the ceiling. The smoke rose up through every crack, every duct, every open door, through elevator shafts and stairwells. Escaping into the open air, the smoke rose in a column nearly one mile high. . . . By the time the fire was out, 85 people had lost their lives.

Kerkorian and his partners and their insurance companies paid approximately seventy-five million dollars to the families of the victims. Some thought the tragedy marked the end of the MGM Grand. But just eight months after the fire, the hotel-casino reopened on July 29, 1981—and the steady stream of gamblers returned.

Five years later, Kerkorian and his partners sold this first MGM Grand to Bally's Manufacturing Company for $440 million in cash. (Bally's also took over $110 million in company debt.) Kerkorian kept the rights to the name MGM Grand, and for a reason. He was already planning, once again, the largest hotel, casino, and theme park built up to that time and was ready to risk something between $750,000,000 and one billion dollars on this new MGM Grand.

Again, he won.

Kerkorian "knows exactly the right price to buy or sell," observed Larry Woolf, who headed the new casino. "When the price is right, it's Win, Win, Win! No risk. Zero. Zip."

Not everyone shared Kerkorian's confidence in the time before the profits began rolling in. But a young man who first saw Las Vegas when he was ten years old later joined Kerkorian in proving that enormous gambles sometimes pay off.

Lonely Nights

Some nights when young Steve Wynn went to sleep in Las Vegas, his father disappeared from their motel room. Steve realized after a while that Michael Wynn was at one of the Strip casinos, gambling away the money he had earned by running the bingo games at the Silver Slipper.

"He would bet on anything that moved," David Spanier wrote. That visit to Las Vegas ended abruptly. "Within a few weeks, father and son were hitting the road, broke, back to Maryland."

Steve Wynn, who remembers his father fondly as "a kid who never grew up," recalls those troubled days: "When you see a person crumble and lose his self-confidence, it's a very horrible experience. But one thing my father's gambling did was to show me, at a very early age, that if you want to make money in a casino . . . the answer is to own one."

Young Wynn carried away vivid memories of the little town of Las Vegas in the early 1950s: "There was nothing but desert between the Frontier and the Dunes. I used to go horseback riding every day in the sand. Everybody was wearing cowboy boots and hats. It was glamorous, it had stars, it had the Mafia. Nobody knew who was who."

He was impressed by the people in the casinos and by the business itself: "I looked at the pit bosses, who wore those high collars . . . and the cocktail waitresses, who were all very beautiful, and I said to myself, what a hell of a business! I was intrigued by a business that offered the glamour of the movies and the stability of a bank."

While attending the University of Pennsylvania, Wynn would return each weekend to help his father operate a chain of Maryland bingo parlors. "Since the day I took my first breath," Wynn said, "I have been a kid who has never had a meal, a dollar for tuition, or a piece of clothing on my back that didn't come from gambling."

Then, in 1963, surgeons discovered that Michael Wynn had a damaged aortic valve and attempted to repair it. He died on the operating table.

"My world collapsed that day," Wynn said years later. But the death taught him something important: "I've never been afraid of anything since."

After his father's death, Wynn took over the bingo parlors—but in 1967 he made his way back to the Las Vegas he remembered, ready to change the town forever.

The Helpful Banker

While he was still in his twenties, Wynn met a man who was ready to bet on his future. This was E. Parry Thomas, head of the Valley Bank, who loaned him enough money to buy a liquor distributorship.

Liquor wasn't the business Wynn wanted to stay in, but it provided a small grubstake. With his modest profits, and helped by a sizable loan from Thomas, he made his first major investment in Las Vegas. Acting through intermediaries, Wynn managed to persuade Howard Hughes to sell him a small parking lot next to Caesars Palace for $1,100,000. When Caesars heard that Wynn might be thinking of opening a competing casino on the lot, it paid him $2,250,000 for the property.

With his personal profit from that sale, he was ready to move into the world that had first attracted him to the town. His first project was reconstructing one of the earliest—and most neglected—Downtown casinos—the Golden Nugget.

Soon after he began buying stock in the Golden Nugget, he discovered that the casino's money was "slipping through the cracks." Spanier writes: "A bar owner downtown, whom Wynn had once helped out, repaid the favor: he told Wynn that every morning around 3 or 4 A.M. a group of employees from the Nugget—dealers, floormen, shift bosses—met at the bar to divide up 'a ton of cash.' Even the parking attendants were cheating on tickets."

Convinced that the men who were then running the casino were incompetent, Wynn bought more stock, gained control, and set out to make the rundown old casino the showplace of Downtown Las Vegas. Within a year the Golden Nugget's profits rose from one million dollars to $4,250,000, and by 1977 (after he built a new hotel tower) the figure had jumped to twelve million dollars.

His success there gave him the cash he needed for a major gamble. Wynn bought an old motel on the boardwalk at Atlantic City, New Jersey, for $8,500,000, tore it down, and then built the 506-room Golden Nugget on the ocean front for $140,000,000.

He felt that the existing Atlantic City casinos were drab and gray and decided he would offer people "a big dose of color." His contribution to the boardwalk included "vaulted, mirrored ceilings, crystal chandeliers, stained glass and marble pillars." He was soon operating the most profitable casino ever built in Atlantic City— even though it was also the smallest.

He was also the first operator of a major New Jersey casino to realize that the days of making easy millions there might be over. Shortly after he reached that conclusion, Bally's—a major casino operator facing a possible unfriendly takeover by the ambitious New York City deal-maker Donald Trump—made a spectacular offer: $440,000,000 for the Golden Nugget. The offer came at a time when the casino "was worth perhaps half that much, given a realistic view of Atlantic City's prospects," Spanier estimates. Wynn accepted the huge offer and headed back home to Las Vegas.

The $630,000,000 Gamble

For fifteen years, Nevada casino owners had concentrated on increasing their profits from their existing properties in Las Vegas. Then, in 1988, Wynn began building the Mirage—the most elaborate and expensive casino ever constructed up to that time—on a 102-acre site next to Caesars Palace.

His new project featured an atrium nine floors high and a special habitat for the rare royal white tigers bred by Siegfried and Roy. As guests lined up to register, they could watch sharks, rays, surgeonfish, and triggerfish swimming in a twenty-thousand-gallon salt aquarium just behind the reception desks. And Wynn's architects had already begun planning a carefully designed "marine environment" where visitors could get a close look at the world's most expensively maintained dolphins. The eventual cost of that addition was fourteen million dollars.

Wynn had decided to offer a special attraction to the very small number of enormously wealthy gamblers who roam the world, sometimes risking as much as a million dollars during their brief visits to a casino. He spent around twenty-four million dollars to construct and furnish eight luxurious villas for these high rollers.

Other casinos had offered elaborate suites, but Wynn spoke of his two-bedroom and three-bedroom villas as "residences." A Mirage press release described what his favored guests would find:

Upon entering the foyer a beautifully crafted glass dome highlighted with gem-like crystals reflects a rainbow of light across rich imported wall fabrics and inlaid marble floors. European art from the 17th, 18th, and 19th centuries lends grace to the ambience of this private entry. . . . The formal living room offers intimacy and comfort on the grandest scale. Sunlight streams through ten foot tall French doors drenching this incomparable salon in a sea of light. Hand-loomed carpets center a luxurious seating area in front of a marble fireplace. . . . A crystal chandelier and elegant dining table provide a romantic setting in which to enjoy world-class cuisine prepared exclusively in the private villa kitchens. . . . Each bedroom has been created in a scale reminiscent of a 17th century royal chateau. . . .

High rollers responded by coming in much larger numbers than Wynn had anticipated.

"I thought there might be a hundred players worldwide who could bet as much as a million dollars," Alan Feldman, vice president of the Mirage, recalled. But about six weeks after the Mirage opened, Wynn asked one of the officers to print out a computer list of players who had bet a million or more on a single visit to the new casino.

"He holds up this list," Feldman said. "On each page there's 20 names. And he let it go. There were 20 pages. Four hundred names."

Since the house ends up with something between 14 and 20 percent of the amount risked by each gambler, it is possible for a casino to gain as much as $1.2 million from a single gambler who shows up six times a year to risk a million dollars on each visit.

Some experts who did not realize how many high rollers the Mirage was attracting were convinced that this time Wynn had gone too far. After investing $630,000,000, he would have to take in at

Pirate Fantasy: Steve Wynn's Treasure Island resort recreates the atmosphere of Robert Louis Stevenson's adventure novel without neglecting the details of a modern casino. While gamblers try their luck at the tables and slot machines inside, casual strollers along the sidewalk outside can see a realistic sea battle on Buccaneer Bay. The Show is free. (Mirage Resorts)

Steve Wynn set new standards for Las Vegas in the Polynesian atmosphere of the Mirage, then surpassed them all with plans for an even more luxurious new resort. Here he seems delighted with a tabletop model of Bellagio before the opening in 1998. (Mirage Resorts)

"I like Las Vegas. Admittedly, it is relentlessly vulgar, noisy, money-grubbing, deceitful and repetitive. Granted it screams bad taste from slot parlor to tower block, from gilded faucet to mirrored bedroom, inside and outside . . . glitz without end. . . . Despite all that, I like it. . . . The point about it, which both its critics and admirers overlook, is that it is wonderful and awful simultaneously. So one loves it and detests it at the same time."
—David Spanier, *Welcome to the Pleasuredome*

least a million dollars a day just to cover expenses, they estimated. A few predicted early disaster for the new venture.

"You can't make a nut [daily operating expenses] of a million-plus a day with that set-up," one experienced casino executive said. "The ratio of staff to guests is too high, the costs are enormous, Wynn's borrowed up to his eyeballs."

Actually, the Mirage was profitable from the first month and came out ahead even during the usually very slow month of December. The cash flow for the first year was close to $200 million.

Two years later, with the Mirage now the most successful casino in the world, Wynn and his partners began planning another major addition to the Strip—the 2,900-room, $430,000,000 Treasure Island, inspired by Robert Louis Stevenson's novel. To draw visitors to the themed casino, Wynn staged an elaborate outdoor show on

"Buccaneer Bay," featuring a dramatic battle between a full-sized pirate ship and a British man-of-war.

In previewing Treasure Island just before the opening, Ann Henderson reported in *Nevada* magazine: "On each side, 15 professional stuntmen will shoot it out and do all that buccaneer stuff, like falling overboard. One of the ships is hit by cannon fire and sinks. The winner? The pirates—after all, this is Vegas."

With more than a billion dollars still at risk in the Mirage and Treasure Island, Wynn might be expected to relax, enjoy his extraordinary good luck, and count his millions. Instead, he began sketching out his most ambitious project, which seemed likely to cost twice as much as the Mirage.

The Riverside was the first of a cluster of thriving casinos built in a once-deserted spot that became Laughlin, Nevada, a popular vacation town on the Colorado River. (Las Vegas News Bureau)

THE SATELLITES

From the cockpit of his little Comanche 250, Don Laughlin looked down at a silvery bend in the Colorado River and liked what he saw. After taking off from Las Vegas one morning in 1964, he had followed the course of the river from Hoover Dam to Davis Dam, soaring above crumpled desert and skinny Lake Mohave to South Point, a half-forgotten spot ninety miles south of the Las Vegas Strip. There, on the west bank of the river, near the southernmost tip of wedge-shaped Nevada, he intended to build the casino of his dreams.

Anyone less imaginative than Don Laughlin might have seen just a lonely roadside diner called "Mike's Camp" and an abandoned eight-room motel surrounded by blowing dust and tumbleweed. Not a human figure in sight. At the desert crossroads where Nevada meets California and Arizona, summer temperatures could climb as high as 120 degrees Fahrenheit—hot enough to roast travelers in their cars. Who would want to spend more than five minutes here? But Don Laughlin smiled. What he saw was his air-conditioned future, bright with colored lights and prosperity.

More than thirty years later, Laughlin surveys his domain from the top of the newest tower in his thriving Riverside Resort. Through floor-to-ceiling windows of his penthouse on the twenty-eighth floor, he has a clear view of Colorado River traffic: sightsee-

"When U.S. 95 almost runs out of Nevada, Laughlin suddenly appears on a side road in the Colorado River Valley, in a startling blaze of electricity. Laughlin exists for gambling. Casinos, one after the other, dominate the main street and the riverbank. . . . Neon lights start to come alive at twilight; the glows that emerge create a nightlife of their own."
—Sheila Swan and Peter Laufer, *Neon Nevada*

ing boats filled with tourists, pleasure boats pulling adventurous water-skiers, ferryboats shuttling back and forth from the Arizona side. Laughlin's own tour boat, the U.S.S. *Riverside,* is pulling away from the dock. On a typical day it will carry a wedding party or a business group on a charter cruise.

Two miles upriver, cars and campers from everywhere are streaming across the bridge connecting Bullhead City, Arizona, with Laughlin, the Nevada town named for its founder. This is the bridge that Don Laughlin built with three-and-a-half million dollars of his own money. Then he gave it to the two states, Nevada and Arizona. On the Nevada side, cars swing into Casino Drive and head for parking lots adjoining the Riverside and a string of other casinos and resorts, most of them owned by corporations. Across the street from the Riverside, Don Laughlin's 900-unit RV park is filling up with vacationers in campers, trailers, and motor homes.

Every night, all night, the Colorado River lights up with shimmering reflections of this desert Monte Carlo. Names of the casinos flash in colored lights, beckoning gamblers to the Colorado Belle, Flamingo Hilton, Edgewater, River Pines, and all the others. Swarms of visitors fill more than ten thousand hotel rooms. More arrive daily at the new airport with its 7,500-foot runway, just across the river in Bullhead City.

Don Laughlin owns most of the airport buildings. He also owns subdivision property behind the airport, a bank in Laughlin, and a sixty-thousand-acre cattle ranch near Kingman, Arizona. His private helicopter waits on its Riverside rooftop pad, ready to take him anywhere he wants to fly, any time. Laughlin is a skillful pilot with a commercial license that gives him freedom to move between his several properties in Arizona and Nevada.

In the years since he bought that boarded-up motel and six acres of desert land, Don Laughlin's success has been phenomenal. The

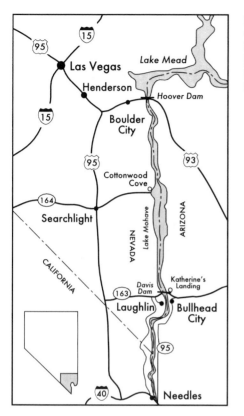

Laughlin, Nevada, on the west bank of the Colorado River, is ninety miles south of Las Vegas, near the southern tip of the state. (Location Map: Laughlin/Las Vegas area)

town of Laughlin has grown to become the third busiest gambling destination in Nevada, outranked only by Las Vegas and Reno. Its popularity has inspired other Las Vegas spin-offs, east and west of the city, but Laughlin remains the biggest of the satellites, the only one started from scratch. If all this prosperity grew out of one man's optimistic imagination, it may have begun when Don Laughlin was a schoolboy in Owatonna, Minnesota.

Bells and Colored Lights

Looking back, Laughlin recalls the cheerful sound of bells and the flash of colored lights from slot machines in neighborhood taverns around Owatonna. When he was about ten years old, he liked to go to the taverns with his mother. Pinball and slot machines were tolerated in Minnesota at the time, and young Don was fascinated by them. By the time he was in the ninth grade, he had found a way to buy his own slot machine.

Thumbing through a magazine, Don came upon an ad that offered the first step in his business career. Slot machines, he discovered, were for sale by mail. If he could only raise enough money to order one, he felt sure he could make it pay for itself. And the best way to raise money in Owatonna, he believed, was to trap enough wild minks and muskrats to sell to furriers. So he began to spend long, frozen mornings and afternoons hunting the animals along creeks and rivers outside of town.

Very soon the boy had made enough money from animal pelts to send for his first slot machine. Before long he was in business, installing pinball and slot machines in Owatonna's bars and taverns, raking in about $500 a week—a small fortune in the 1940s. But when he was a fifteen-year-old high school sophomore, Don Laughlin was called to the principal's office to hear an ultimatum.

"You'll have to make a choice," said the principal. "You can give up the slot machines or leave school!"

So Laughlin left school. Today, he says he has never looked back. Five years later, at twenty, he was on his way to Las Vegas with his young bride. With some money from his Minnesota enterprise, he bought a small bar in North Las Vegas and installed the flashiest slot machines he could find. In the mid-1950s he sold the bar and enrolled in dealer school. Eventually he bought the 101 Club in North Las Vegas and made it profitable, but his dreams were bigger

"I used to trap mink when I was a kid. During the war, when all the men were gone, there wasn't anybody trapping. One winter I trapped forty-five mink, and they were worth between twenty and forty dollars each. That money was pretty big then. So I made a lot of money when I was just nine or ten years old."
—Don Laughlin

than that. By 1964 he was looking for new opportunities. That's when he discovered "Mike's Camp," the derelict diner and motel on the west bank of the Colorado River.

The diner had opened in the 1940s to serve construction crews at work on the Davis Dam. Across the river in Arizona, a new town was growing up around the main camp. Workers named it Bullhead City for Bull's Head Rock, an oddly shaped cliff used as a navigation point by steamboat captains in earlier days.

Up and Down the River

As early as 1857, sternwheelers had chugged up the river from the Gulf of California to Fort Mojave, near the present location of Bullhead City, bringing supplies to the fort or picking up ore from nearby gold mines. Riverboat travelers could book passage from the fort to San Francisco for forty-four dollars.

"I built the 101 Club in North Las Vegas and opened it in 1954. (Now it's called The Opry House.) It was always a successful operation, so when I sold it in '64 I had the money to negotiate a deal with the owners of the place on the river. I got a license right away. Back then you could get a license in two or three months. Now it would take two or three years. You know the rest of the story. . . . We've been under construction ever since."—Don Laughlin

In those days, the Colorado River could be dangerous and unpredictable. Intermittent floods caused havoc along the banks. Even as far away as the Imperial Valley of California, where irrigation water traveled through canals from the Colorado, farmers dreaded every spring thaw in the distant mountains. When the Bureau of Reclamation was established by the federal government in 1902, flood control was one of its goals. Between 1905 and 1907, when devastating floods wrecked much Imperial Valley farmland, reclamation engineers were sent to study strategic sites for dams along the Lower Colorado.

Dr. Arthur Powell Davis, commissioner of reclamation at that time, suggested that a huge dam would not only control the floods but would also store precious water for settlements in several southwestern states. Pyramid Canyon, now the site of Davis Dam, was among seventy possible sites studied, but the engineers selected Black Canyon, sixty-seven miles upriver, as the ideal site for the ambitious Boulder (Hoover) Dam project described in Chapter 4. When Hoover Dam was completed in 1935, the Bureau of Reclamation once more turned its attention to Pyramid Canyon. The dam built at that site would be named for Arthur Davis, still known to reclamation engineers as the father of the Boulder Canyon Project.

A construction contract for Davis Dam was awarded in 1942, but the work was interrupted because of material shortages during World War II. After the war, dam builders returned to work and the dam was completed in 1951. Its primary purpose was to regulate the flow of the Colorado River and provide water for households and farms downstream, as far south as Mexico. Once the dam was up and running, South Point camp was abandoned. Except for occasional fishermen or curious travelers venturing off the main roads between Los Angeles and the Grand Canyon, nobody had any reason to go there—until thirty-three-year-old Don Laughlin took a look at the place and saw its possibilities.

Across the river from the empty motel, Bullhead City had become a permanent Arizona settlement. A few government workers had chosen to stay there in the 1950s, after their jobs on Davis Dam ended, and other retirees eventually followed them, attracted by the sunshine and the river. The town was still growing. Surely, Laughlin reasoned, local fun-seekers would welcome a new and different place for relaxation and entertainment. And, since gambling was illegal in Arizona, a casino across the river would bring Las Vegas–style diversion within easy reach. By 1966, Laughlin's brand-new Riverside Casino was open. Customers were lining up in a parking lot on the Arizona side, waiting for the free ferry service.

It was a small, informal operation at first. Visitors could play on twelve slot machines or challenge fortune at two gaming tables. An "all-you-can-eat" buffet provided chicken dinners for ninety-eight cents. The old motel had been refurbished, offering four rooms for guests. The other four were the Laughlin family's living quarters. Curious day-trippers poured in from Bullhead City, then from as far away as Kingman and Flagstaff. Californians arrived from nearby Needles, then others turned up from more distant cities like Barstow and San Bernardino.

Soon Laughlin's success attracted other entrepreneurs who built their own bars and casinos along the riverbank. The first of these was the Bobcat Club, opened in 1968 and sold in 1972 to an ambitious newcomer, Oddie Lopp. The new owner remodeled and expanded the Bobcat and called it the Nevada Club. Following Laughlin's example, he built a parking lot on the Arizona side of the river and offered ferry service to customers and workers. A third casino, the Monte Carlo, had joined the lineup in 1971, and other operators were beginning to show interest in the Nevada riverbank.

New Town on the Map

The place had no post office and no official name until 1977. All mail deliveries to the Riverside had to be made through Searchlight, a once-prosperous gold mining town about thirty-five miles to the northwest. When a postal inspector advised Don Laughlin to give the place a name, Laughlin suggested Riverside or Casino.

"Too common," said the inspector. "What's wrong with calling it Laughlin? That's a good Irish name!" As Don Laughlin remembers it, the inspector's name was O'Neill. So the U.S. Post Office put up a sign for Laughlin, Nevada.

By 1975 the Riverside had one hundred rooms, the Monte Carlo had become the Crystal Palace, and Lopp's Nevada Club was bustling. These trailblazers were soon joined by the Colorado Hotel (now the Pioneer Club), the Regency, and the original Colorado Belle. A building boom in Laughlin was about to begin. Within ten years, the Riverside occupied two fourteen-story towers and shared the riverbank with a glittering lineup of hotel casinos.

Las Vegas investors, impressed by the success of the Riverside, bought the old Colorado Belle and tore it down to build the more ambitious Edgewater, opened in 1981. Two years later, Circus Circus bought the Edgewater, expanded it, and announced plans for a newer and bigger Colorado Belle next door. When it opened in 1987, the new Colorado Belle was a sensation. Designed to resemble a real Mississippi River side-wheeler, the new hotel-casino had more than two hundred staterooms on the stationary "boat" and a thousand more hotel rooms in a separate tower. Five restaurants catered to hungry travelers. If visitors wanted to see the river from a boat that moved, they could go down to the dock and board the *Little Belle.*

On the other side of Casino Drive, Ramada Express opened in 1988, the only resort not directly on the river. A narrow-gauge railroad with a steam-driven passenger train carried sightseers around the Ramada property. Meanwhile, the Colorado Hotel had been replaced by the Pioneer Club and Gambling Hall, owned by the Santa Fe Corporation, and the old Bobcat/Nevada Club had changed hands several times. By 1988 it had become Steve Wynn's Golden Nugget Laughlin, an elegant resort owned by Mirage Resorts, Inc.

Upstream from the Golden Nugget, the Gold River looked down from a cliff, and Harrah's Laughlin was the only local casino with a sandy beach for swimmers and sunbathers. The name of Laughlin began to turn up on national television weather reports as "the hottest spot in the nation," with summer temperatures consistently above a hundred degrees.

The Laughlin casino boom continued into the nineties. When the Hilton Corporation wanted a piece of the action, it spent $190 million to build the largest hotel-casino in town. Right next door to Don Laughlin's Riverside, the Flamingo Hilton opened in 1990 with two thousand hotel rooms and six restaurants. Not to be outglitzed by the newcomer, Laughlin added a new twenty-eight-story tower to the Riverside in 1994. At the far end of Casino Drive, Bay Shore Inn had opened two years earlier, and other ventures were in the works.

Over the years, since the first three casinos opened on the Nevada shore across from Bullhead City, only one of them failed to keep pace with the speedy growth of the town. The old Monte Carlo motel-casino, renamed Crystal Palace in 1977, closed as a casino in 1985. The motel stayed open until 1990, then it too was closed. Don Laughlin bought the property in 1993 and reopened the motel, but the casino remained closed.

A more successful survivor was the little Regency casino, tucked away between the Flamingo Hilton and the Edgewater. Its owner, Bud Soper, opened the Regency without hotel rooms in 1980 and was content to keep his operation simple and small. The Regency remained on the Laughlin strip.

As the riverbank filled up with hotels and casinos on the Nevada side, Bullhead City became the fastest-growing community in Arizona, housing most of the casino workers who commuted to Laughlin. Between 1980 and 1996, its population grew from ten thousand to twenty-eight thousand. Some of the newcomers were retirees from other places who came to Laughlin for fun and found they liked the climate and loved the river enough to move to Bullhead City.

By 1996 there was room for them in Laughlin, too. A real town was growing behind Casino Drive, with houses and condominiums, a school, a library, a medical center, and a brand-new shopping mall with an underground parking garage. A water treatment plant, on the hill behind the new City Hall, promised enough drinking water for all the hotel rooms, households, and businesses, with

Davis Dam holds back and regulates the Colorado River's flow at Bullhead Canyon, creating skinny Lake Mohave and producing electricity for Southern California. (Nevada Historical Society)

enough left over for expansion. A multi-million-dollar flood control project opened up 250 more acres for development in the city.

Just twenty years after the U.S. Post Office gave the place its name, Laughlin had become a town with its own legends. Riverboat tour guides repeated these legends every day to boatloads of visitors, sometimes embellishing them with colorful details. The story of Don Laughlin's discovery of the old diner was told over and over, with a few details varying according to the storyteller.

October 8, 1964: President Lyndon Johnson signed the act that formally established the Lake Mead National Recreation Area—3,000 square miles of water and desert including Lake Mohave. Created by Davis Dam as a storage reservoir for Colorado River water, Lake Mohave became a year-round mecca for boaters and campers.

The Legend of Mrs. Lafferty

Another much-repeated bit of Laughlin lore is a favorite with riverboat guides. In the words of Captain Pete Roberts of Harrah's *Del Rio* tour boat, here is what one group heard as the boat was passing the Edgewater: "If you'll look up at the tower at the top of the Edgewater, you'll notice a balcony under the last five windows on that top floor. That was a private apartment when they built it.

"There was a lady by the name of Mrs. Lafferty who had a house trailer on about an acre right between the Edgewater and the Colorado Belle. When Circus Circus started to build the Colorado Belle they tried to buy her out, offered her $250,000 for it and she turned it down. Then they offered her $500,000 and she still turned it down. Finally, they offered her a *million* dollars and she turned that down, too."

As Pete Roberts tells the story, the casino builders were desperate to capture that strategic piece of land, but Mrs. Lafferty seemed adamant. They had no choice but to start building around her trailer—until somebody came up with an offer she couldn't refuse.

Some storytellers insist that Mrs. Lafferty said she didn't much like casinos, anyway, so the offer had to be spectacular. When Circus Circus suggested two-and-a-half million dollars, they also sweetened the offer with a few extra trimmings. How would she like a ten-room penthouse—with room service, bar service, and limousine service for the rest of her life? Mrs. Lafferty said she'd like it a lot. So the casino representatives added one more incentive. If she'd move out of her trailer right away, they'd put her up in a suite on the sixth floor of the Edgewater Hotel while they built the tower. The lady accepted, graciously, and her possessions were gently transferred from the trailer to her temporary quarters.

Building the new tower took about a year. During that time, according to Pete Roberts, here's what happened: "She picked out all kinds of antique furniture, took a couple of cruises, came back all set to move in. The sad part of it is, she was eighty years old, and she passed away about a week before they finished the tower. So she never did get to live up there. Her daughter got the furniture and the money, and Circus Circus got the apartment back. They still don't rent it out. They use it for their executives from Las Vegas. . . . Now there's a street named for her, out in the parking lot, called Lafferty Lane."

Bright Lights on the Reservation

In the Paiute language, *avi* means "money" or "loose change." When the Fort Mojave Indian Tribe opened Nevada's first Native American casino on its reservation in 1995, the name seemed just right for a brand-new fifty-six-million-dollar hotel-casino with more than 300 rooms, 700 slot machines, gaming tables, a sports book, and a keno lounge. Just a few miles downriver from Laughlin and Bullhead City, the reservation is a close neighbor on both sides of the Colorado River. A bridge built by the tribe to connect the Arizona and Nevada shores provides a quick route from Bullhead City to the south end of the Laughlin strip. When Avi added its bright lights to the shoreline, it became the first casino reached by cars crossing that bridge.

Nevada's former Lieutenant Governor Bob Cashell, no stranger to casino operations, signed a pact with the Fort Mojave Tribe to run Avi with its 550 to 600 employees. Under the agreement, at least 30 percent of these workers must be Native American.

When Avi opened, it was the only Indian-owned gaming business in the United States to be operated under state regulations. The casino does not pay the usual Nevada gaming tax but is expected to give the Nevada Gaming Control Board 1 percent of its revenue. For the Fort Mojave Tribe, Avi became the first step in an ambitious development plan. On four thousand acres, with three and a half miles of riverfront, the tribe expected to build a community for forty thousand residents. They announced plans for a golf course, a marina, and another casino.

Later Moons in the Las Vegas Orbit

By the mid-nineties, two smaller Las Vegas satellites were growing fast, catching travelers in both directions as they passed through the southern tip of Nevada on Interstate 15. At State Line, forty-five miles southwest of Las Vegas, and in Mesquite, seventy-seven miles northeast, new casinos and resorts were thriving. The casinos were relative newcomers, but each place could trace a much earlier history.

"State Line"—not to be confused with the northern Stateline at Lake Tahoe—didn't show up on Nevada maps in the 1920s, but thirsty travelers knew it was there during the early years of Prohibition. They knew they could find refreshment in the desert on Highway 91 at Whiskey Pete's State Line Station, a two-pump gas station attached to a saloon with a rowdy reputation. It

Whiskey Pete's hotel casino at Primm, Nevada, preserves the legend of a cantankerous bootlegger who dispensed liquid cheer at his State Line saloon during Prohibition years. (Las Vegas News Bureau)

was run by a cantankerous bootlegger by the name of "Whiskey Pete" McIntyre.

The original Whiskey Pete died in the 1930s, but his legend was preserved and embellished. The brawling bootlegger, it was said, had asked to be buried standing up with his hat, gun, and a jug of homemade booze at his feet. His buddies tried to comply with his wishes, but it wasn't easy to dig a hole deep enough for an upright wooden casket. So they slanted it a little, allowing Pete to face the highway that became Interstate 15. When casino pioneer Ernest Primm built a small hotel-casino at State Line in 1977, he named it Whiskey Pete's and continued the legend.

In the summer of 1994, *Nevada* magazine published a new revelation: "The final resting place of the real-life Whiskey Pete McIntyre has been a mystery since his death 60 years ago," wrote associate editor Carolyn Graham. "That is, until last February, when construction crews working near Whiskey Pete's Hotel-Casino at

State Line accidentally kicked up an old coffin. The bones are thought to be those of Whiskey Pete, the trigger-happy bootlegger who ran a gas station at State Line."

Graham's piece ended with a note that Primadonna Resorts, Inc., had plans to rebury Whiskey Pete's bones with a memorial on a nearby hilltop.

Even as late as 1996, when State Line had three big casino resorts with nearly four thousand employees, the AAA tour book listed Whiskey Pete's, Buffalo Bill's, and the Primadonna Resort (given two stars each) under "lodgings" in Jean, a town about fifteen miles from the Nevada-California border. A location for the three establishments was pinpointed "adjacent to I-15, State Line exit." Officially, the place had no name.

Primadonna Resorts, owner of all three casinos at State Line, wanted to call the town "Primadonna." Company lawyers submitted a formal request for the name change to the Clark County Board of Commissioners and also made a gift to the county of a piece of land to hold a local fire station. When the county board

"In 1951, my father, Ernest Primm, acquired 800 acres of rocky, barren desert land at the Nevada border. Today it's home to three resorts . . . (and) the world's tallest and fastest roller coaster. . . . So, it was only fitting that the State of Nevada recently changed the name of the town from the ordinary 'State Line' to Primm, after the man who saw amazing things blooming where even the barley he tried to grow could barely take root."—Gary Primm, CEO, Primadonna Resorts, Inc., in a letter dated November 21, 1996

Primm Valley Resort is the first stop for many travelers crossing into Nevada at Primm, a town named for the late Ernest Primm whose Primadonna Resorts also built Whiskey Pete's and Buffalo Bill's. (Las Vegas News Bureau)

supported the name change, Primadonna lawyers took the next step, submitting their request to state and federal boards on geographic names.

Nearly a year later, on December 3, 1996, Nevada Governor Bob Miller unveiled a brand-new interstate sign at the place formerly known as State Line. "Primadonna" had been turned down as a place name, but the new town would be called Primm, Nevada.

Whiskey Pete is still there—in spirit—presiding over a Wild West hotel with 777 rooms, three restaurants, and a 700-seat showroom. Across the road, a more sedate Primm Valley Resort (formerly the Primadonna) offers turn-of-the century decor in its 660 rooms, or informal service in a neighboring RV village. Next door, Buffalo Bill's beckons thrill-seekers to an amusement park featuring "The Desperado," advertised as "the world's tallest and fastest roller coaster," along with Ghost Town Motion Theater and Adventure Canyon, a log flume ride.

Buffalo Bill's latest thrill ride, opened in 1997, is the Turbo Drop, a 45-mile-an-hour plunge to earth. Adventurous (or foolhardy) droppers have described the sensation as "like flying straight toward the ground in a jet fighter." For more down-to-earth vacationers, the Primm Valley Golf Club offers a 6,945-yard, 71-par course set among seven lakes. The three resorts have a total of 2,600 rooms in Primm.

From Hometown to Boomtown

On the other side of the state, where Interstate 15 cuts through a corner of Arizona to Utah, Mesquite has been a rest stop for travelers since it began as a Mormon farming community in 1895. As one of a string of settlements established by the Mormon Church between Salt Lake City and the Pacific Coast, Mesquite made the trip

easier for travelers by horseback or stagecoach from St. George, Utah, to towns in Southern Nevada.

"Travelers usually planned their journeys through the Virgin Valley to avail themselves of the lodging and ample meals provided by the Mormon families along Mesquite's Main Street," retired Clark County Surveyor James L. Scholl wrote in the *Nevada Historical Society Quarterly*. "With the development of the automobile and paved roads, many of these part-time tourist accommodations evolved into full time businesses."

Tourists didn't stay long in Mesquite, so the population remained small. In *The WPA Guide to 1930s Nevada* (first published in 1940 as *Nevada: A Guide to the Silver State*), Mesquite is described in just four lines as "a trade center of a ranching country settled by Mormons in 1880 on the bank of the Virgin River. It was abandoned a few years later but resettled by Mormons in 1895."

In the 1930s, before World War II, there were 512 residents

"Fun-shine and Sun-shine at the Silver State Gateway" is the slogan adopted by the Mesquite Area Chamber of Commerce. A promotion letter sent to businesses in 1997 describes the attractions of Mesquite, "the fastest growing city in Nevada . . . surrounded by picturesque mountains to the south and breathtaking mesas to the north. . . . If the hospitality isn't enough to capture your heart, then how about the fact that Mesquite offers the lowest tax rate in Nevada."

in Mesquite. By 1997 the town had grown to 1,900, but that figure did not begin to reflect dramatic changes in the face of the town. In the late 1990s it had become a bustling resort destination with casinos, golf courses, RV parks, and entertainment. While casinos on the east and west ends of town filled with tourists, residential neighborhoods in the middle seemed to preserve the quiet flavor of a small western community.

"Even with its scanty population," Scholl wrote, "Mesquite's strategic location on Interstate 15 . . . made it an ideal site to build a resort casino. In 1981, the Reno-based Peppermill Resort Hotel and Casino recognized Mesquite's economic potential and purchased the Western Village truck stop."

Western Village, at the time, was a motel on the west side of town with twenty-eight rooms, a coffee shop, and a gas station. Over the next ten years, Peppermill expanded it into The Oasis, a 700-room hotel with four restaurants, six swimming pools, and a golf course. That was just the beginning of Mesquite's transformation.

Meanwhile, on the east side of Mesquite, the Virgin River Hotel and Casino opened in 1991, the same year that saw the opening of a new high school and a plastics manufacturing plant. Four years later, the Oasis had changed hands and had become Si Redd's Oasis Resort Hotel Casino with an adjacent ninety-one-space RV park and another golf course. On the new map of Mesquite City, the Oasis Golf Course covered almost as much space as the city itself. The Virgin River Hotel doubled its number of rooms.

Near the Oasis, a new eighty-million-dollar resort opened in June 1995. Players Island Resort-Casino-Spa brought the town another golf course and five hundred more hotel rooms, along with restaurants, convention facilities, entertainment, and more jobs. Television entertainer Merv Griffin was the major stockholder. By 1997, Holiday Inn had opened its new Rancho Mesquite Casino, adding one more vacation possibility for gamblers. But maybe casino resorts in Mesquite had reached a saturation point, at least temporarily. By 1998 Player's Island was in trouble. In July that year, the new resort was bought by a group of individual investors (incorporated as RBGLLC) and became CasaBlanca. Under its new name, CasaBlanca expanded along with the town and became part of the civic-minded Mesquite Resort Association.

This Mormon town had always been more than a Las Vegas satellite. As a hometown, it continued to grow. A brand new airport was in the works for the new century. Less than eighty miles away, the big city of Las Vegas was growing as a hometown, too.

"A Nevada neon hunt is a nighttime activity. The desert night sky and a two-lane road, punctuated with occasional neon signs, create a mood unique to Nevada. Often the only lights for hours are the constellations and a few passing cars—until far off in the distance there is an electric flicker that suggests some form of civilization on the horizon."—Sheila Swan and Peter Laufer, *Neon Nevada*

Fantastic shapes rise out of the desert, constantly changing the Las Vegas skyline. Glimpses of Paris, New York, and Camelot are sprinkled among giant hotel towers as the Strip keeps on growing. (Las Vegas News Bureau)

THE SPREADING OASIS

"You gotta know when to hold 'em—know when to fold 'em . . ."

The amplified voice of Kenny Rogers greets newly arrived travelers as they hurry toward the moving walkways at Las Vegas McCarran International Airport. In the air, more voices: Bill Cosby, Debbie Reynolds, Joan Rivers, and a succession of current headliners seem to be passing the microphone from hand to hand on an invisible stage, reminding travelers to watch their luggage . . . stand on the right . . . hold on to the children . . . put out that cigarette.

Carried along by the magic carpet, travelers move into the atrium of a neon-lit terminal and disperse toward escalators or glass elevators, heading for baggage carousels, car-rental counters, and taxis. They're not all tourists and conventioneers. Many are here to work in hotel-casinos on the Las Vegas Strip. Others have jobs in offices, hospitals, classrooms, or industries. A few have lived here all their lives. Their faces—in all shades—reflect a mixture of international origins.

Outside the terminal, waiting for taxis, newcomers survey the city skyline—surprisingly close—across a narrow strip of desert. From travel brochures they recognize a few fantastic shapes—an Egyptian pyramid, a medieval castle, and what looks like the Statue of Liberty—set among new towers and a forest of building cranes. What they don't see from here is the growing city beyond the Strip. On the outskirts, whole neighborhoods are springing up in places that used to be empty desert.

"Try riding a plane to Las Vegas and listen to the people talk. It's all optimism and euphoria—because something *might* happen."
—Anthony Curtis, *Las Vegas Adviser*

"In a little more than half a century, casino gambling helped transform a barren little whistle-stop into one of the most glittering resort cities in the world."
—Eugene Moehring, *Resort City in the Sunbelt*

Colored lights illuminate the Las Vegas sky at night, beckoning travelers to come in and explore glittering casinos and hotels. (Las Vegas News Bureau)

Shrinking Desert: On the outskirts of the city, new neighborhoods seem to sprout overnight, adding new streets, new houses, new schools and churches to a sprawling metropolitan Las Vegas. Even young residents remember when these areas were empty desert. (Las Vegas News Bureau)

In these neighborhoods, the ring of hammers heralds the building of new houses, new schools, churches, supermarkets, and shopping centers. Planned communities—some with golf courses, club houses, tennis courts, and day-care centers—draw affluent new residents. Some of these neighborhoods are established and growing, some still on the drawing board, but all are being filled as new residents arrive every day.

Who Lives in Las Vegas?

In the early 1990s, as many as six thousand people were moving into Las Vegas and Clark County every month. In the fastest-growing city of the nation's fastest-growing state, builders were racing to keep up with the demand for new houses to shelter families moving in from other parts of the country. Later in the decade, with the building of more and more new resorts and casinos on the Las Vegas Strip and around the city's periphery, workers continued to move in to staff the hotels and to build houses for newcomers like themselves.

"The growth is enormous!" said Irene Porter, executive director of the Southern Nevada Home Builders Association. "Look at all the new casino properties that just opened. Thousands of new jobs. Those are NEW jobs! And those people have to have somewhere to live."

Hotel and casino workers aren't the only newcomers to Las Vegas. The demand for more housing means more construction jobs and more newly arrived construction workers to fill them. Those workers need housing, too.

"A lot of these construction workers tend to stay on in Las Vegas," said Porter. "They like the climate, they find they can work twelve months out of the year, and the wages are good—in many

"I can still remember when I was a kid just walking around here barefooted, looking for rattlesnakes and walking up and down the creek and jumping in the pool that used to be down there at this old Stewart Ranch in the early days of Las Vegas . . . and going to school and knowing everybody at school."—Ed Von Tobel Jr., Las Vegas businessman

Passing through McCarran International Airport, thousands of travelers arrive in Las Vegas every day. More than thirty million were counted in a single year. Some have come to stay. (Las Vegas News Bureau)

"The Las Vegas of the fifties and sixties was a small town. . . . It was one of those mythical places where front doors were left unlocked and there were more churches per capita than anywhere else in America."—Alan Richman, "Lost Vegas," from *Gentlemen's Quarterly,* November 1992

cases better than where they came from. Besides, the work is more consistent and more plentiful."

Some of the new houses are lived in by military families stationed at Nellis Air Force Base, just outside Las Vegas. As other bases around the country closed in the 1990s, Nellis was expanding. Since there wasn't enough housing on the base for all the new people, many of them settled in city suburbs and commuted to Nellis. Many of these Air Force families will become permanent residents. Over the years, the city has become a favorite retirement spot for military people. Some of them retire young—in their forties—and go on to second careers in Nevada businesses.

Thousands of nonmilitary couples, too, come to Southern Nevada to retire. Attracted by the warm climate, vigorous economy, and the absence of a state income tax, they build homes or move into retirement communities. Young families choose neighborhoods with conveniently located schools and parks. When the children are ready for college, they may consider the University of Nevada, Las Vegas, where more than twenty thousand students enroll every year.

"Grand Old Ivy"

Some of these students pursue traditional degrees in arts and sciences, but many come to UNLV to study hotel management or performing arts or the economics of gaming and entertainment. Part-time jobs on the Strip give them first-hand experience. Student archaeologists and paleontologists don't just examine prehistoric fossils, they uncover them in the neighboring deserts.

As a university, UNLV has a very short history. Until 1969 it was called Nevada Southern College, an extension of the University of Nevada, Reno, which was founded as a land-grant college in 1874. In Las Vegas, the first college classes were offered in 1951 during a postwar building boom. Nevada historian Eugene Moehring traces the establishment of the college to a 1950 petition from Nellis Air Force Base to the University in Reno for extension classes in Clark County. In *Resort City in the Sunbelt,* Moehring explains why, after first refusing, the University regents finally agreed: "The military, in a surprise move, contracted with the University of Southern California for the classes. New pressure came from teachers in Clark County's rapidly expanding school districts for advanced courses to fulfill state requirements. Fears that either southern California- or Utah-based universities would eventually invade southern Nevada prompted the board to take action. In 1951, the University of Nevada went beyond the concept of extension courses and instituted a formal program in Las Vegas."

"When I moved to Las Vegas in the early 1950s, there were headlines in the paper: 'Las Vegas is running out of water!' They said it would never grow any bigger . . . and that was when it was 25,000 people. They had a few casinos on Fremont Street. That was all. And they thought they were running out of water. . . . Now it's almost a million people and they're still building."
—Don Laughlin, 1996 interview

Moehring's history describes in detail the political maneuvering and dedicated fund-raising that led to the growth of Nevada Southern. The first bachelor of arts graduates received their degrees in 1964. Within another decade the college was firmly established as the University of Nevada, Las Vegas.

Today the UNLV campus covers 335 acres in an academic neighborhood off South Maryland Parkway. Most of the buildings are less than forty years old—no ivy-covered halls—yet there's a feeling of quiet permanence mixed with youthful enthusiasm on the campus. Tree-shaded walks lead from one modern building to the next. The oldest structure, Maude Frazier Hall, opened in 1957 as headquarters for the small college. Now UNLV employs more than six hundred faculty members and offers at least a hundred graduate and undergraduate programs.

For part-time students who want to take short, intensive workshops or after-hours classes to fit busy work schedules, the Community College of Southern Nevada (one of the largest community colleges in the nation) provides a full catalog of possibilities and the only public planetarium in Southern Nevada. This branch of the University and Community College System of Nevada operates three campuses—in Las Vegas, North Las Vegas, and Henderson—where more than 27,000 students come and go. The eighty-acre Health Sciences Center in Las Vegas specializes in health-care education.

When Las Vegans need medical attention they can find it quickly, including hospitals and emergency services listed in the Yellow Pages. If they're looking for religious houses of worship, they'll find more than five hundred of them representing forty faiths, from African Methodist and Baha'i Faith to Greek Orthodox and Sikh. Traditional Protestant and Catholic churches are visible in neighborhoods throughout the city, along with synagogues and Jewish temples. The largest number of churches are Mormon

(Church of Jesus Christ of Latter-day Saints)—a reminder that Las Vegas began as a Mormon mission.

Hometown Recreation

Once they've settled in, families find plenty to do away from work and school. Music lovers soon discover the Las Vegas Symphony Orchestra and Nevada Opera Theatre. Ballet fans gravitate to the Nevada Dance Theatre. Drama buffs find the Las Vegas Little Theater, New West Theatre Company, and the Rainbow Company theater for children. Newcomers interested in the visual arts, history, science, or nature can find museums devoted to their special enthusiasms.

Children quickly adopt the Lied Discovery Children's Museum, where they can make a test run through life—as a doctor, actor, broadcaster, painter, musician, astronaut, or computer scientist—in a single morning or afternoon of role-playing. Inside the eight-story Science Tower they bend sound waves, test weather instruments, or create light displays.

For the whole family, hiking, horseback riding, rock-climbing, camping, swimming, boating, and fishing are within easy reach. Many neighborhoods have tennis courts and golf courses. The Lake Mead National Recreation Area is less than an hour away, and Red Rock Canyon National Conservation Area is even closer.

In winter, skiers find snow-covered slopes and ski lifts atop Mt. Charleston, just thirty-five miles from the desert city where summer temperatures routinely soar above 100 degrees. For air-conditioned recreation any time, there's an ice-skating rink, roller skating, bowling, and virtual-reality game centers—not to mention all the glittering attractions of the Strip.

Without leaving their cars, sightseers on Las Vegas Boulevard can survey more than five miles of fantasyland before deciding

"Casino profits fueled a real estate boom which built a city of endless condominiums, elegant townhouses, and posh country clubs—a landscape of Spanish mission elegance to complement the spa-like image of the city's recreational economy. Even the cheaper apartments bordering the Strip, for low-income workers unable to afford a car, rated far above the housing for their counterparts in the garden state."
—Eugene Moehring, *Resort City in the Sunbelt*

"There is nothing garish here, nothing glitzy. . . . The new Strip skyline—snaking from downtown all the way to the airport—has become part of the new show that is Las Vegas."—Gaye Delaplane in the *Reno Gazette-Journal,* October 25, 1998

Shaped by time and erosion over a billion years of geologic change, red and white sandstone strata have become a sculpture garden in the Valley of Fire, Nevada's first state park. (Las Vegas News Bureau)

At Lake Mead National Recreation Area, less than an hour away from the city, Las Vegas boaters can sail in open water or explore hidden coves along more than seven hundred miles of shoreline. (Las Vegas News Bureau)

where to stop for a closer look. New York City, Ancient Egypt, or King Arthur's Camelot? How about a tropical jungle where tigers roam free, or a pirate village in a Caribbean cove? Then there's the lavish Roman world of the Caesars, right there at the corner of Flamingo Road and Las Vegas Boulevard.

"All these classic images from all of Western civilization!" journalist Michael Ventura commented in 1996. "It's as though Western history had come here for one last party."

The Glory That Was Rome

When Caesars Palace opened in 1966, it was decades ahead of its time—the first of a series of sumptuous "theme" hotel-casinos that eventually would dominate the Las Vegas Strip. Designed for adult tastes in the days when the Strip seemed to ignore the existence of families with children, Caesars is still a fantasyland for grown-ups. But now young visitors come with their parents to sample non-gambling diversions.

In The Forum Shops at Caesars, a city-size shopping mall, families stroll along Roman pavements under changing Mediterranean skies, past ornate fountains and frescoed façades of classical buildings with very modern store windows. They shop for clothes, books, jewelry, or gadgets; buy an ice cream cone or a meal; pause at the Festival Fountain to watch hourly performances by animated statues of Roman gods. Inside the casino, they visit the domed Omnimax Theatre for an hour or so of exotic travel on a panoramic movie screen surrounding the audience.

Under the Big Top

"Family entertainment" was an expression not heard on the Las Vegas Strip until Jay Sarno, creator of the opulent Caesars Palace,

Bottlenose dolphins are year-round residents at the Mirage, where they view with curiosity the visitors who parade through their outdoor habitat. Some baby dolphins were born here. (Mirage Resorts)

tried something entirely different. Starting small in 1968, two years after Caesars made its splashy debut, Sarno's Circus Circus was promoted as "the first gaming establishment in the world offering entertainment for all ages." Sarno died in 1984, too soon to see the Circus Circus Hotel and Casino expand into a complex of towers dominating a sixty-nine-acre site on the Strip at Sahara Avenue, with bargain hotel rooms and a Circusland RV Park always filled with motor homes and campers.

In the summer of 1993, Circus Circus opened Grand Slam Canyon, a ninety-million-dollar indoor theme park covering five acres inside an enormous transparent pink dome. "Canyon Blaster," a rollercoaster with dizzying double-loops and steep drops, zoomed around and above the climate-controlled amusement park, where winding paths led to other thrill rides. A few gentler rides were sprinkled among play areas for small children, where animated dinosaurs allowed themselves to be petted.

More, More, MORE Theme Resorts!

Three years earlier, Circus Circus Enterprises had introduced a fanciful new silhouette to the Las Vegas skyline at the southwest corner of Tropicana Avenue and Las Vegas Boulevard. Excalibur, a turreted 4,000-room hotel-casino, was built to resemble a medieval castle. As soon as the castle lowered its drawbridge for the first time, families with children became a common sight on the Strip. Crowds streamed across the bridge to watch Merlin's magic and King Arthur's Tournament, to relive legends of knights and ladies in Camelot. With this $260-million theme resort, Circus Circus Enterprises became a formidable power on the Strip.

Two months after the 1993 debut of Grand Slam Canyon, Circus Circus Enterprises staged another grand opening. Next door to Excalibur, a thirty-story glass pyramid rose out of the desert. Beyond an avenue of royal palms, a larger-than-life-size sphinx guarded the entrance to Luxor, the corporation's most lavish resort at the time. Named for the Egyptian city of Luxor on the Nile, near the site of ancient Thebes, Luxor Las Vegas was designed around Egyptian themes, with obelisks and hieroglyphics and a full-size replica of King Tut's Tomb. A powerful searchlight beam reached ten miles into the night sky from the top of the pyramid.

Lure of the South Sea Islands

Long before the success of Excalibur and Luxor sent other entrepreneurs scurrying to dream up new theme resorts, a luxurious adult playground was luring high-rollers to Steve Wynn's Mirage. From the day it opened in 1989, right next door to Caesars Palace, this Polynesian paradise lured nongambling tourists as well.

Attracted by waterfalls and grottos and jungle greenery in the middle of a small lagoon, they crowded onto the sidewalk in front of the casino, then trooped inside to stroll through groves of real banana palms and tropical vines in a nine-story rain forest. They marveled at the coral-reef aquarium and the habitats for bottlenose dolphins and Bengal white tigers. After dark they moved outdoors to watch the manmade volcano erupt in a shower of fireworks every fifteen minutes until midnight.

Within four years, Mirage Resorts, Inc., had opened a second theme resort on the 102-acre site where Steve Wynn had become King of the Strip. This time, the theme was drawn from Robert Louis Stevenson's pirate adventure *Treasure Island*. Visitors loved it, whether they gambled or not. Any passerby could step off the public sidewalk onto a wooden dock in front of Treasure Island to watch eighteenth-century pirates battle British sailors on "Buccaneer Bay." No tickets were needed.

Treasure Island was an undisputed success with families. Newspapers and magazines around the world ran pictures of the pirate battle to illustrate stories about the "new" Las Vegas, a child-friendly place where families could find plenty of wholesome entertainment. True . . . but casino executives protested that children were not the main focus of the new resorts.

"Las Vegas is an adult destination," said Mirage vice president Alan Feldman in 1993. "It has been for the better part of sixty years and will be an adult destination for as long as any of us can see into the future. What's going on in Las Vegas right now is a change, to be sure. There *are* more kids. If people want to bring their kids to the Mirage, we've got tigers and dolphins and fish and a rain forest and lots of kid things for them to do. They can have a fantastic time here, but this is an adult vacation resort."

A few years later, as more theme resorts and amusement parks were added to the Strip, Feldman saw no reason to change his mind. "The media loved the novel idea of kids in Las Vegas," he said, "but I think they missed the whole point when they wrote about 'family entertainment in a city for gamblers.' Las Vegas is not *just* about gambling. It's about *fantasy*. People come here to play act."

Feldman has his own memories of youthful fantasies fulfilled in Las Vegas. "When I was twenty-two," he recalled, "I brought a girl-friend to Las Vegas from Los Angeles . . . and we got all dressed up and went to the Portofino Room at the Desert Inn. . . . As God is my witness, I WAS James Bond! Those one-dollar chips were a hundred thousand dollars, and that was Doctor No across the table. . . . I think that happens to millions of people who come here."

The Yellow Brick Road

As sightseers found new wonders to explore on the Strip, Las Vegas residents often joined them. Across the Strip from Excalibur and Luxor, a giant golden lion crouched at the main entrance to Kirk Kerkorian's billion-dollar MGM Grand Hotel/Casino—City of Entertainment. Between the lion's paws, a yellow brick road enticed crowds into a vast complex of emerald green glass, where characters from the Wizard of Oz set the Hollywood theme.

Opened just before Christmas in 1993, the whole MGM property spread across 112 acres. With more than five thousand hotel rooms and suites, a huge assortment of convention and sports facilities, and a mini-Disneyland (with no gambling) out back, the MGM Grand set a record at the time as the "world's largest hotel, casino and theme park." Before the complex was five years old, MGM Grand, Inc., was at work on plans to make it even bigger by the turn of the century.

Skeptics wondered if Las Vegas had overdone its expansion, but developers continued to announce plans for more growth. The success of a mile-long monorail between the MGM Grand and Bally's–Las Vegas led to speculation about a future monorail system linking all the major resorts on the Strip to McCarran International Airport and the Las Vegas Convention Center.

Soon there would be even more theme resorts, on and off the Strip. Behind the scenes, casino corporations perfected their plans for new wonderlands with thousands of hotel rooms to be filled with conventioneers, gamblers, wedding parties, and vacationing families. As more and more visitors arrived to fill those rooms, some skeptics had second thoughts. New casino projects created new jobs and workers poured in from around the world, looking for places to live. More houses, more construction, more jobs. Before the end of the century, the number of people living in Clark County would grow to an estimated 1,250,000 — more than a third of the entire population of Nevada. And they were sharing their hometown with 32 million visitors a year.

Where the Glitter Began

Downtown on Fremont Street, the original Glitter Gulch spruced up its shopworn image and opened as the Fremont Street Experience in December 1995. Seventy years after a thin coating of asphalt made it the first paved street in town, Fremont Street had become a landscaped pedestrian walkway covered by a ninety-foot-high canopy. Between refurbished casinos on either side of the street, crowds gathered every night to watch animated images created by millions of colored lights on the inner surface of the canopy. A changing program of computer-generated music and light shows filled Fremont Street with dancing color and stereophonic sound.

Back on the Strip, more new casinos were ready to open in 1996. The long-delayed Stratosphere Tower, 1,149 feet tall, finally made it in April. With a revolving restaurant, observation decks, and "the world's highest roller coaster" at the top, it is the tallest building west of the Mississippi River. After years of speculation about his financial problems, Stratosphere originator Bob Stupak had sold the property to Grand Casinos, Inc., of Minneapolis.

Monte Carlo, recalling the historic Place du Casino in Monaco, opened its ornate doors at the south end of the long block between Flamingo and Tropicana Avenues. Mirage Resorts and Circus Circus, in a successful collaboration unprecedented on the Strip, had combined their resources to build the Monte Carlo near the construction site of Steve Wynn's ambitious Bellagio. When that opulent resort opened in 1998, the two casinos were linked by a tram railway.

Magic was definitely in vogue on the Strip. Illusionist Lance Burton performed in his own theater at the Monte Carlo; Siegfried and Roy were permanent attractions at the Mirage; Merlin, King Arthur's wizard, starred at Excalibur; Spellbound was a regular feature at Harrah's; other magicians headlined at smaller casinos, and David Copperfield appeared regularly at Caesars Palace. Then, three days before the Monte Carlo opened with Lance Burton, Caesars launched the biggest magic show in town. Caesars Magical Empire showcased dozens of illusionists as waiters, guides, and entertainers in a new Roman-atmosphere complex with multiple theaters, private dining rooms, and catacombs.

The facelift wasn't finished yet. Before the end of 1996, Orleans opened on Tropicana Avenue west of the Strip, bringing Mardi Gras and the French Quarter to Las Vegas. Then the new year, 1997, began with the long-heralded opening of New York–New York, a $344-million theme resort created jointly by MGM Grand and Primadonna Resorts. The new complex at the corner of Tropicana Avenue and Las Vegas Boulevard offered visitors a chance to sample the Big Apple without leaving the Strip. Behind a replica

"The newest way to make an impression on the garish Las Vegas Strip is through Impressionism itself. The Bellagio, a luxury hotel being built in a city known for its girlie shows, clanging slot machines and the Liberace Museum, will have hallways graced by about $130 million worth of paintings by the likes of Renoir, Monet and Picasso. . . . Las Vegas is adding a little elegance to its ebullience, a little class to its crass."
—Andrew Pollack in the *New York Times*, November 13, 1997

"Picasso was a lusty Spaniard. Picasso belongs in a casino."
—Steve Wynn on the Charlie Rose TV show, May 20, 1997

of the Statue of Liberty, New Yorkers recognized a dozen familiar outlines, such as the Chrysler and Empire State Buildings, as they strolled through Central Park, Times Square, Coney Island, and Greenwich Village.

A few blocks away, Harrah's had changed its image from Mississippi riverboat to tropical beach, where live bands played Latin rhythms and jazz. Multicolored palm trees shaded La Playa, an indoor-outdoor lounge. Down the street, on twenty-four acres next to Bally's, the Hilton Corporation began building a new theme resort to be called Paris. A fifty-story replica of the Eiffel Tower would be the centerpiece of this latest travelogue casino, where a visitor could walk through a smaller Arc de Triomphe and along the Champs Elysées to sip coffee at a sidewalk cafe.

Hilton had taken over Bally's Entertainment Corporation and was ready to expand. At the big Las Vegas Hilton, next door to the city's convention center, *Star Trek* enthusiasts awaited the debut of "StarTrek: the Experience," a joint venture of The Hilton Hotel Corporation and Paramount Parks. As soon as it opened, Trekkies were reliving imaginary *Star Trek* adventures inside a virtual-reality complex.

How Much Is Too Much?

As building cranes multiplied along the Strip, cautious Las Vegans protested the exploding growth. UNLV historian Hal Rothman told a television interviewer: "I have a developer friend who says that there will be two million people in this valley in the year 2010. If he's right, I don't want to be here."

Boulder City author Dennis McBride was even more pessimistic: "Las Vegas is coming in . . . for a very, very rude awakening and some serious disaster in the next decade if they don't get a control

The Stratosphere Tower is the tallest building west of the Mississippi River, rising 1,149 feet into the air and providing a beacon for lost motorists between Downtown and the Strip. (Las Vegas News Bureau)

over their growth. . . . I mean, you can sit in the Mirage and have your five dollar cup of coffee or take a skiff out on the Bellagio Lagoon and climb to the Stratosphere Tower and look at the Las Vegas Valley, but you don't realize that if it weren't for the water, it would be impossible to have anything like that. And that water is coming to an end."

McBride's warning was broadcast in a December 1996 television documentary about Las Vegas. An unseen narrator explained that Nevada's water allotment, granted in 1922 by the Colorado River Compact, was "infinitesimal compared to her present-day needs. As compared to Southern California at 4.4 million acre feet of water, and Arizona at 2.8 million, Nevada only gets one third of a million acre feet a year. That's less than the estimated amount of water that evaporates from the Colorado River every year. But the city with nearly 100,000 hotel rooms keeps on guzzling 325 gallons per person, per day."

McBride considered remedies. "Las Vegas is trying to find other sources of water," he said. "Are we going to drain the Virgin River? Are we going to steal the ground water from Nye County and the other rural counties? Are we somehow going to have the Colorado River Compact rewritten so we can get more water out of the Colorado River itself?"

Governor Bob Miller had no immediate answers but said he received dozens of suggestions for bringing water to the desert, including a plan to pipe water from the Pacific Ocean, "bringing it across the desert, taking care of L.A. on the way. . . . All these things are feasible. They're just very, very costly."

Comedian Alan King seemed undisturbed. "Vegas has nothing to worry about," he insisted. "Las Vegas is unique, and I think it'll just grow and grow."

Journalist/novelist Michael Ventura was less optimistic: "In the year 2100, I see a sea of sand out of which the Stratosphere Tower sticks up . . . lonely, deserted. And people who come in the year 10,100 will ask, 'What were these people doing here? Why did they build that tower? It must be religious.'"

Undeterred by pessimists, the builders kept on building. The innovative Steve Wynn introduced a diplomatic note of caution at a 1997 news conference when he suggested, "In our growth policy, we should focus on quality." His own elegant Bellagio, inspired by an Italian village overlooking Lake Como, opened in October 1998 behind its own eight-acre lake. Fountains in the lake performed nightly for strollers along the Strip, stopping traffic on the sidewalks. Crowds surpassed those attracted by the Mirage volcano and the sea battle at Treasure Island.

Circus Circus Enterprises had destroyed the old Hacienda Hotel, south of Tropicana, in a dramatic implosion to celebrate the New Year 1997. Two years later, a new forty-two-story casino resort had risen on the site. In collaboration with Four Seasons Hotels, Circus Circus had opened Mandalay Bay with enough big-name entertainment to satisfy Broadway buffs, baby boomers, and opera fans. Onstage in the 1700-seat Mandalay Bay showroom, Chita Rivera and Ben Vereen starred in *Chicago,* the full-length musical straight from Manhattan. Sixties icon Bob Dylan turned up at midnight to open the House of Blues at Mandalay Bay, and operatic tenor Luciano Pavarotti arrived a few weeks later to fill 12,000 seats in the Mandalay Bay Event Center for a one-night performance.

Not to be upstaged, the even newer Venetian Resort-Hotel-Casino announced, shortly before its 1999 opening, that Madame Tussaud's Wax Museum in London would have a Las Vegas branch at the Venetian. The *New York Times* had already pronounced the Venetian

"Bellagio opened to the public shortly before 11 P.M. on October 15 (1998) preceded by an invitation-only, black-tie party. The Las Vegas Review-Journal reports 80,000 people visited Bellagio during its first 18 hours of operation."—*Las Vegas Linage,* from Las Vegas News Bureau, November 1998

"At the far end of the Conservatory is the Gallery of Fine Art, housing $300 million worth of Impressionist, 19th- and 20th-century masterpieces. . . . Plan to spend 40 minutes to an hour there, especially if you want to hear taped information, narrated by Wynn, on all 27 art pieces in the collection." —Gaye Delaplane in the *Reno Gazette-Journal,* October 25, 1998

Bellagio, Steve Wynn's latest upscale resort on the Las Vegas Strip, has its own lagoon, three thousand hotel rooms, and a treasury of original paintings from around the world. (Mirage Resorts)

the "grandest of all" casinos on the Strip, and the Las Vegas News Bureau called it "the largest privately owned facility of its type in the U.S." Built by Sheldon Adelson on the former site of the legendary Sands, once a playground for Sinatra's Rat Pack, the new theme resort was designed to give visitors a taste of romantic Venice, with canals and singing gondoliers. Its six thousand hotel rooms were ready, ahead of time, to house revelers at Millennium parties already being planned to usher in the New Year 2000.

Down the street, a movie-set Eiffel Tower and Arc de Triomphe reminded Strip explorers that Paris, too, had become part of a Las Vegas itinerary. What could casino developers do for an encore? There were rumors of a Titanic resort, based on the ill-fated ocean liner, to be built on the Strip with 1,000 hotel rooms adjoining a replica of the ship.

When the city celebrates its one-hundredth birthday in 2005, there may be a few guests at the party who remember Las Vegas as it was not so long ago—a dusty little railroad town. But the big resorts on the Strip will be ready for fireworks, special effects, and unprecedented surprises—the kind of Las Vegas celebration the world has learned to expect.

"Las Vegas is a party that never stops," says Steve Wynn. "God bless this daffy place!"

You wonder
what you'll do
when you reach
the edge
of the map

Out there
on the horizon

All that neon

Beckoning you

In from the dark

—Kirk Robertson, "Driving to Vegas" in *Just Past Labor Day*

New York–New York Hotel & Casino—a joint venture of Primadonna Resorts and MGM Grand, Inc.—adds some familiar Big Apple silhouettes to the Las Vegas skyline. (Las Vegas News Bureau)

MORE ABOUT LAS VEGAS . . .

Selected Bibliography

Books and Articles

Arrington, Leonard J. *The Mormons in Nevada.* Foreword by Mike O'Callaghan. Las Vegas: *Las Vegas Sun,* 1979.

Balboni, Alan. *Beyond the Mafia: Italian Americans and the Development of Las Vegas.* Reno: University of Nevada Press, 1996.

Barber, Phyllis. *And the Desert Shall Blossom.* Salt Lake City: University of Utah Press, 1991.

———. *How I Got Cultured: A Nevada Memoir.* Reno: University of Nevada Press, 1994.

Bartlett, Donald L., and James B. Steele. *Empire: The Life, Legend and Madness of Howard Hughes.* New York: W. W. Norton, 1979.

Brown, Joseph E. *The Mormon Trek West: The Journey of American Exiles.* Photos by Dan Guravich. Garden City, N.Y.: Doubleday, 1980.

Castleman, Deke. *Las Vegas.* Oakland: Compass American Guides, 1993.

———. *Nevada Handbook.* 5th ed. Chico, Calif.: Moon Publications, 1998.

Daughters of Utah Pioneers. *The Las Vegas Fort.* Salt Lake City: International Society of Daughters of Utah Pioneers, 1994.

Davis, Sammy, Jr., with Jane and Burt Boyar. *Why Me? The Sammy Davis, Jr., Story.* New York: Farrar, Straus and Giroux, 1989.

Demaris, Ovid. *The Boardwalk Jungle.* New York: Bantam, 1986.

Drosnin, Michael. *Citizen Hughes.* New York: Holt, Rinehart and Winston, 1985.

Dunar, Andrew J., and Dennis McBride. *Building Hoover Dam, An Oral History of the Great Depression.* New York: Twayne Publishers, 1993.

Egan, Ferol. *Frémont, Explorer for a Restless Nation.* Reno: University of Nevada Press, 1985.

Elliott, Russell R. *History of Nevada.* 2d ed. Lincoln: University of Nebraska Press, 1987.

Fiero, G. William. *Geology of the Great Basin.* Reno: University of Nevada Press, 1986.

———. *Nevada's Valley of Fire.* Las Vegas: K.C. Publications, 1985.

Frémont, John Charles. *Report of the Exploring Expedition to the Rocky Mountains in the Year 1842 and to Oregon and North California in the Years 1843–44.* Washington: Gales and Seaton, 1845.

Graham, Jefferson. *Vegas: Live and In Person.* New York: Abbeville Press, 1989.

Greenwood, Earl, and Kathleen Tracy. *The Boy Who Would Be King.* New York: Dutton, 1990.

Guralnick, Peter. *Last Train to Memphis: The Rise of Elvis Presley.* Boston: Little, Brown and Company, 1994.

Harrington, Mark R. *Ancient Tribes of the Boulder Dam Country.* Pamphlet. Las Vegas: Clark County Historical Society; Los Angeles: Southwest Museum, n.d.

Highton, Jake. *Nevada Newspaper Days: A History of Journalism in the Silver State.* Stockton, Calif.: Heritage West Books, 1990.

Hulse, James W. *Forty Years in the Wilderness: Impressions of Nevada 1940–1980.* Reno: University of Nevada Press, 1986.

———. *The Nevada Adventure.* 6th ed. Reno: University of Nevada Press, 1990.

Lillard, Richard G. *Desert Challenge: An Interpretation of Nevada.* Lincoln: University of Nebraska Press, 1966.

McBride, Dennis. *Building Hoover Dam: An Oral History of the Great Depression.* Boulder City, Nev.: Boulder City/Hoover Dam Museum, 1993.

———. *In the Beginning: A History of Boulder City, Nevada.* Boulder City, Nev.: Boulder City/Hoover Dam Museum, 1992.

———. *Midnight on Arizona Street: The Secret Life of the Boulder Dam Hotel.* Boulder City, Nev.: Boulder City/Hoover Dam Museum, 1993.

McCracken, Robert D. *Las Vegas: The Great American Playground.* Reno: University of Nevada Press, 1997.

Malone, Michael P. *The Battle for Butte: Mining and Politics on the Northern Frontier, 1864–1906.* Seattle: University of Washington Press, 1981.

Maxon, James C. *Lake Mead–Hoover Dam.* Las Vegas: K.C. Publications, 1980.

Moehring, Eugene P. *Resort City in the Sunbelt: Las Vegas, 1930–1970.* Reno: University of Nevada Press, 1989.

Moody, Bill. *Death of a Tenor Man.* New York: Walker and Company, 1995.

Paher, Stanley W. *Las Vegas: As it began—As it grew.* Las Vegas: Nevada Publications, 1971.

———, ed. *Nevada: The Official Bicentennial Book.* Las Vegas: Nevada Publications, 1976.

Puzo, Mario. *Inside Las Vegas.* New York: Grosset & Dunlap, 1967.

Reid, Ed, and Ovid Demaris. *The Green Felt Jungle.* New York: Pocket Books, 1974.

Roske, Ralph J. *Las Vegas: A Desert Paradise.* Tulsa: Continental Heritage Press, 1986.

Scholl, James L. "Mesquite Nevada: From Farm Hamlet to Resort City 1880–1995." *Nevada Historical Society Quarterly* 38, no. 2 (summer 1995): 89–103.

Smith, John L. *Las Vegas.* Las Vegas: K.C. Publications, 1995.

Spanier, David. *Inside the Gambler's Mind.* Reno: University of Nevada Press, 1994.

———. *Welcome to the Pleasuredome: Inside Las Vegas.* Reno: University of Nevada Press, 1993.

Stevens, Joseph E. *Hoover Dam: An American Adventure.* Norman: University of Oklahoma Press, 1988.

Stegner, Wallace. *The Gathering of Zion: The Story of the Mormon Trail.* New York: McGraw-Hill, 1964.

Stout, Hosea. *On the Mormon Frontier: The Diary of Hosea Stout, 1844–1861.* 2 vols. Edited by Juanita Brooks. Salt Lake City: University of Utah Press; Utah State Historical Society, 1964.

Strong, Emory. *Stone Age in the Great Basin*. Portland, Oreg.: Binfords & Mort, 1966.

Swan, Sheila, and Peter Laufer. *Neon Nevada*. Reno: University of Nevada Press, 1994.

Taylor, Richard B. *Laughlin, Nevada, History Book*. Vols. 1 and 2, newspaper clippings and city documents, compiled and published by Richard B. Taylor, 1988.

Thomas, Bob. *Liberace: The True Story*. New York: St. Martin's Press, 1987.

Titus, A. Costandina. *Bombs in the Backyard: Atomic Testing and American Politics*. Reno: University of Nevada Press, 1986.

Torgerson, Dial. *Kerkorian: An American Success Story*. New York: Dial Press, 1974.

Wiley, Peter, and Robert Gottlieb. *Empires in the Sun: The Rise of the New American West*. New York: G. P. Putnam's Sons, 1982.

WPA. *The WPA Guide to 1930s Nevada*. Foreword by Russell R. Elliott. Reno: University of Nevada Press, 1991.

Documentary Sources

Berman, Susan, Melissa Jo Peltier, and Jim Milio. *Las Vegas: Gamble in the Desert*. Script for MPH Entertainment, Inc., television documentary aired December 1996.

————. *Las Vegas: House of Cards*. Script for MPH Entertainment, Inc., television documentary aired December 1996.

Las Vegas News Bureau, *Las Vegas Linage,* monthly news releases, 1994–98.

Oral Histories

Cahlan, John F. *Fifty Years in Journalism and Community Development: An Oral History*. Interview by Jamie Coughtry, 1987. University of Nevada Oral History Project. Special Collections, University of Nevada, Reno, Library.

————. *Reminiscences of a Reno and Las Vegas, Nevada, Newspaperman, University Regent, and Public-Spirited Citizen*. Interview by Mary Ellen

Glass, 1968. University of Nevada Oral History Project. Special Collections, University of Nevada, Reno, Library.

Dunbar, Leo, et al. *Hoover Dam and Boulder City, 1931–1936: A Discussion Among Some Who Were There.* Moderated by Guy L. Rocha and R. T. King, 1985. University of Nevada Oral History Project. Special Collections, University of Nevada, Reno, Library.

Godbey, Erma O. *Pioneering in Boulder City, Nevada.* Interview by Mary Ellen Glass, 1966. University of Nevada Oral History Project. Special Collections, University of Nevada, Reno, Library.

Rockwell, Leon H., *Recollections of Life in Las Vegas, Nevada, 1906–1908.* Interview by Mary Ellen Glass, 1968. University of Nevada Oral History Project. Special Collections, University of Nevada, Reno, Library.

Ullom, George L., *Politics and Development in Las Vegas, 1930s–1970s.* Interview by Jamie Coughtry, 1989. University of Nevada Oral History Project. Special Collections, University of Nevada, Reno, Library.

INDEX

Page numbers in italics refer to illustrations

Miller, Bob, 105, 194, 216
Miller, Thomas, 44
Minsky's Follies, xvi
Mirage, The, *155,* 156, 173–74, 176,
    208, 209–10
Miss Atomic Bomb, 113–14
Mob, the. *See* organized crime
Moehring, Eugene, 45, 83, 91, 145,
    199, 203, 205
Mohave, Lake, 6, *188,* 189
Mohave Indians, 10–11, 190–91
monorails, 212
Montana: William Clark and, 38–40
Monte Carlo Resort, *162,* 185, 186,
    187, 213
Moody, Bill, 146
Moore, Terry, 122
Moore, William, 75, 85, 87, 88
Morelli, Hal, *80*
Mormon Fort. *See* Old Mormon Fort
Mormons/Mormon Church, 204–5;
    lead mine operation, 23–25; letters
    of Aroet Hale, 25–26; Mesquite,
    Nev., and, 194; plans for western
    settlement, *19,* 20; relations with
    Paiute Indians, 21, 22, 23, 24–
    25; settlement at Las Vegas, 17–18,
    20–21
Mormon Trail, 20
Moulin Rouge, 146–48
Muddy River, 10
"Murder, Incorporated," 93, 96
mushroom clouds, *108, 112*

NAACP. *See* National Association for the
    Advancement of Colored People

Nash, Alanna, 138
National Association for the
    Advancement of Colored People
    (NAACP), 147–48
National Distillers, 96
National Public Radio, 1, 2–3
Native Americans: Anasazi, 10, 13–15;
    Basketmaker culture, 8–10; casinos
    and, 190–91; early presence of, 4–
    6, 7–8; Mohave, 10–11, 190–91;
    Navajo, 86; Paiute, 9, 11, 21, 22,
    23, 24–25, 27; petroglyphs, 8, *9;*
    slavery among, 11
Navajo Indians, 86
Nellis Air Force Base, 202, 203
Nelson, Phyllis. *See* Barber, Phyllis
    Nelson
Nelson, Tommy, 61, 62
Neon Nevada (Laufer and Swan), 179,
    197
Nevada: atomic bomb testing, xvii,
    108, 109–18, 130–31; control of
    gambling, 75; desegregation and,
    147–48; early indigenous peoples,
    4–6, 7–11, 13–15; Howard Hughes'
    investments in, 129; legalization of
    gambling, xvi, 84; racism in, 146;
    state boundaries, 28
Nevada (magazine), 177, 192–93
Nevada: A Bicentennial History
    (Laxalt), 6
Nevada: A Guide to the Silver State,
    195. See also *WPA Guide to 1930s
    Nevada*
Nevada Club, 185, 186, 187
Nevada Dance Theatre, 205